Jacques Ellul
on Politics, Technology, and Christianity

Jacques Ellul
on Politics, Technology, and Christianity

*Conversations with
Patrick Troude-Chastenet*

Wipf & Stock
PUBLISHERS
Eugene, Oregon

JACQUES ELLUL ON POLITICS, TECHNOLOGY AND CHRISTIANITY
Conversations with Patrick Troude-Chastenet

Copyright © 2005 Patrick Troude-Chastenet. All rights reserved. Except for brief quotations in critical publications or reviews, no part of this book may be reproduced in any manner without prior written permission from the publisher. Write: Permissions, Wipf & Stock, 199 W. 8th Ave., Suite 3, Eugene, OR 97401.

ISBN: 1-59752-266-X

Translated by Joan Mendès France from the French *Entretiens avec Jacques Ellul* by Patrick Troude-Chastenet. Copyright © 1994, Éditions de la Table Ronde, Paris, France

This English translation was previously published by Scholars Press as *Jacques Ellul on Religion, Technology, and Politics:Conversations with Patrick Troude-Chastenet* Copyright © 1998 University of South Florida

*In memory of Jean-Louis Seurin
(1925–1995)*

TABLE OF CONTENTS

INTRODUCTION 1
General introduction.
CHAPTER ONE 19
Provincial. Minority. One book. A world without prospects. The Holy Spirit. Political power. The cold monster. Anarchy and Christianity. Reactionary. Humble words. Environmentalists. A libertarian Marx. New philosophers for the old right. Happiness. Intellectual responsibility. Pessimism and Manicheanism. Non-conformism. Non-violence. Means and ends.
CHAPTER TWO 27
An austere individual. Consecration post-mortem ? Work. Availability. The sin of pride. Specialization. Woe betide the polygraph. Presence in a modern world. Le Pen. Computer science. Socialism. Change revolutions. The Algerian war.
CHAPTER THREE 33
Father. Mother. Genealogy. Origins. An aristocrat. Sense of honour. The Obrenovic's. Malta. The Jewish calender. The Austro-Hungarian Empire. Pierre Mendès France. Political realism. Christians and politics. No war is just. The power of the "bureaux". The Bible.
CHAPTER FOUR 41
Childhood memories. The Jardin Public. A good fight. Secular State schoolboys versus those from private Catholic schools. Friendship. Roaming around. The Bordeaux quays. The navy or the law ? The Arcachon bassin. The canoe. Top of the class. Bordeaux smart society. Cold and calculating. Lead soldiers. The army. An obvious candidate for reform. Unpublished poetry. Introspection. A man like any other. Psychoanalysis.
CHAPTER FIVE 49
The absolute. The Bible. Conversion. A matter between God and myself. School-minded. Goethe. Tacitus. Kierkegaard. Dialectics. Marx. Politics in the lycée. Girls and boys. Law school. Camping in the Pyrénées. Maurice Duverger. The Jèze strikes. A Dutch-looking girl.
CHAPTER SIX 59
Personalism.The Hitler Youth. The Wandervogel. Scout and anti-scout. Bernard Charbonneau. Camps in the Pyrénées. Cult of effort or of pleasure ? At a Nazi meeting. *Esprit*. Emmanuel Mounier. Pioneers of ecology. The Bordeaux branch of the Friends of *Esprit*. Letter to Hitler. The third path. *Ordre Nouveau*. Non-conformists. "Think globally, act locally." The civil war. The power of ideas. Anarchists. George Bataille. The Uriage School.
CHAPTER SEVEN 69

Roman law. The perpetual edict. University career. The *Manicipium*. The *agregation*. Senior lecturer in Strasbourg. Struck off by Vichy. The Gergovian plateau. De Lattre de Tassigny. Back to Bordeaux. Professor on the land. First potato harvest. University's independence. Henri Vizioz. Roger Bonnard. The Resistance. Violence. The National Council for the Resistance. The purge.

CHAPTER EIGHT 77

Bordeaux interim city council. Political parties. A prefect. Christianity and power. Serve and not dominate. A wife's influence. The comedy of power. A deanship. Post war purge. The National Liberation Movement. Elections. A systematic non-voter. The democratic game. Direct democracy. Village life during the Occupation. Mass society. Camping with Charbonneau. Mayor of Pessac.

CHAPTER NINE 85

Places to write. Anarchists. Totalitarian states. Sources. Bernard Charbonneau. Genuine democracy. Professional politicians. The prevention club. Delinquents and community workers. Elections. Political illusion. Sociology and theology. Objectivity in the social sciences. The author and his work.

CHAPTER TEN 91

Living fully. Listening to others. The sensitivity of a woman. The friend and the wife. Bernard Charbonneau and Yvette Ellul. The bone of contention. Mother and daughter. South Africa. Jean-Paul Sartre. Crowds. Bach versus Mozart. I have no regrets. Foreign languages. Morocco. Hassan II.

CHAPTER ELEVEN 101

Freedom of man in the freedom of God. The dilemma of non-believers. The New Jerusalem. Recapitulation. The historical will of man. God is Love. The Word of God. Prophets and false prophets. Democracies and dictatorships.

CHAPTER TWELVE 109

Human nature. Natural law. Incarnation. God. Hell. A possible impossibility. Technology and authority. Pessimism. The man of faith and the man of science. The *exousiai*. God in History. An arbitrary god ? Microcomputing and revolution.

CHAPTER THIRTEEN 117

Technology. Technological society and ecological thinking. Man and nature. Progress. Consciousness raising. A misunderstanding. Political party or counter force ? A more frugal society. The economic programme of the Greens. Genesis.

CHAPTER FOURTEEN 121

Man the guinea-pig. Ambivalence of technological progress. The State and bio-ethics. Voluntary Termination of Pregnancy. The Church and morality. The State faced with miracles. Organ donors. The Bible and blood. The body and eternal life. Gene therapy. Biology and the race struggle. The Church and cloning. Medically assisted pregnancies. *Biological adultery.*

CHAPTER FIFTEEN 129

Bach and Mozart. Léo Ferré. The Threepenny Opera. Delacroix. Michelangelo. Villon. Hugo. Péguy. The empire of nonsense (Art in the technological Society). Dali. Structuralism. Klee. *Guernica*. Art split asunder. Chilling perfection. Art and technology.

NAME INDEX 135

INTRODUCTION

"I describe a world with no prospects, but I believe that God accompanies man throughout his whole existence". This is what Jacques Ellul told me one day. The man who wrote *La Foi au prix du doute* (The price of faith is doubt) died with this certitude on the 19th of May 1994 at his home in Pessac, just a few kilometers from the Bordeaux campus.

Right to the very last his long illness was to provide an illustration of one of his favourite themes namely that of the ambivalence of technological progress. It was to prevent him from completing our last two interviews. He, who used to thank his Maker continually for having given him an iron constitution and computer-like memory suffered agonies at not being able to find the name of this or that poet or painter that he had so loved. In the twilight of his life his body, which he had for so long overlooked, claimed its due forcing itself in a myriad ways into our conversation. My *maître* was made of more than just his great intellect. Having to face this fact left me feeling very uneasy.

I should point out that for more than ten years, no doubt out of a sense of propriety, so-called personal questions, even the usual platitudes about general well-being, had been singularly absent from our conversations. The name [1] of the collection where this book was originally to appear left no doubt as to the biographical nature of the undertaking, but by tacit consent we were constantly putting off the moment when we would leave the work and talk about the man.

It is probably not a coincidence that our relationship took a new turn following the death of his wife on the 16th of April, 1991. From that date on Jacques Ellul's life was never the same again. He was overcome by grief. For a while I thought he may never be able to get over it. He had covered the walls of his sitting-room with photos of his wife, Yvette. This is where he used to receive all his guests. I think he was filled with regret and felt that it was urgent that he bear witness to how important she had been in his life. He wanted to convince me that his wife had shaped his destiny and that without her he would never have achieved his life's work.

I remember once when he handed back the manuscript of an introduction to his ideas that I had written, having conscientiously corrected the misprints and spelling mistakes, like the good teacher that he was, he turned to me and said: "That's good work but you haven't once mentioned my wife." I found this remark rather unjust since I was presenting the work in an academic context, nevertheless I promised to repair the oversight. In fact it wasn't an oversight but a deliberate, admittedly debatable, decision on my part to treat the work without systematically referring to the author's life.

If one is to go by the definition given by the German philosopher Wilhelm Diltey the work of a biographer is firstly to determine the objectives of the subject of the biography and then use these to throw light on how he lived his life and did what he did. There are extremely few lives that actually lend themselves to such a mechanical approach but if one were to apply this method to Jacques Ellul one would have to say that he always wanted to be a free man and a free spirit. Too bad if the word free has become a hackneyed term today ; there is no better word to describe the underlying value that guided Ellul in all fields and in all circumstances.

Ellul cherished this freedom throughout his whole life having received it, as he said, as his father's legacy to him. Just six months before his own death, at an international conference dedicated to his work, Ellul revealed to us that his father had bequeathed him three guiding principles : never lie to anyone including yourself, be charitable towards the weak and stand up to those more powerful than yourself.

Jacques Ellul was born on the 6th of January, 1912 in Bordeaux to Marthe Mendès and Joseph Ellul and was brought up with the aristocratic values of the right. His father was an Italian Serb, from a Greek Orthodox background but Voltarian by conviction. His mother was French-Portuguese and a Protestant. Both parents came from rather grand families that had fallen on difficult times.

After completing his studies in Vienna, Joseph Ellul was taken on as a representative in one of the major trading houses in Bordeaux. He had come to Bordeaux just to acquire a little professional experience and had no idea that he was to meet his future wife there. Being of a somewhat uncompromising frame of mind, he placed his notion of honour above everything, as a consequence of which he was to find himself thrown out of work on several occasions.

To make ends meet his wife Marthe taught art at a private school and also gave painting lessons at home. According to Ellul's description of his childhood he was studious, poor but happy.

When he was at the lycée de Longchamp he was top of the class. So once his home-work was finished his mother would let him rove off to his heart's content spending whole afternoons on the quays, the river banks and exploring the marshlands in Eysines. Of an evening before supper the young Ellul would delve into the Bible for stories of the Hebrew people which he revelled in. On Sundays and holidays he would learn foreign languages from his father who was a polyglot, or indulge in a rather unusual activity for someone who was to be so anti-military. He loved painting the uniforms on his lead soldiers always being careful to respect the historical details.

The family lived quite close to the Jardin Public, and it was there that he and his classmates from the state school would wage battles of heroic proportions against the boys from the private Catholic school. He obtained his baccalauréat at the lycée Montaigne at the early age of sixteen having always excelled in Latin, French, German and History.

His passion was the sea, he dearly wanted to become a naval officer but his father made him read law. When he went up to the University of Bordeaux in 1929, he was already on his way towards total conversion to Christianity having experienced the presence of God in circumstances that he had never wished, out of modesty, to describe. The definitive nature of his Christianity took some time to develop.

During the academic year 1929-1930 he was to make a second important encounter this time through the Protestant Student Federation. He began a lasting friendship with a former school mate who at first sight seemed to have absolutely nothing, but nothing, in common with Ellul.

Sixty years later, Bernard Charbonneau can still recall pacing up and down rue Fondaudège with his friend all evening long [2]. Each one of them was trying to bring the other round to what he considered to be the important issues. For Ellul, this was belief in God. For Charbonneau [3], it was the *Grande Mue* (The Great Moulting Process), in other words the radical change in the human condition caused by the rise of science and technology.

With hindsight it is interesting to note that these two young men, scarcely out of adolescence had intuitively identified the subjects that were to be their lifetimes' preoccupation and production. Their work proceeded in parallel and sometimes in collaboration. If Charbonneau's work has so far not achieved acclaim, Ellul never failed to acknowledge his debt to the author of many of his ideas. He maintained that without the help of this very gifted friend, who taught him *how to think*, he would never have discovered what the technological phenomenon really entailed.

Bernard Charbonneau summed up his own project by saying that he wanted to analyse the consequences of the scientific and technological revolution on man, which he investigated through the prism of his two contradictory and inseparable passions : nature and liberty. Indeed he blamed technological progress for having drastically disrupted both natural order and liberty as well as disturbing the dialectic relation that bound the two together. Ellul's system followed exactly the same lines, with God in the place of Nature.

Although Ellul's conception of liberty along Christian and Barthian lines differs from that of Charbonneau's personal and agnostic approach, liberty lies at the heart of both their thinking. In both cases liberty is seen in terms that are so totally different from abstract ideas defined according to philosophical categories. Liberty is perceived as a constant struggle between an individual and the perils that constantly beset him : scientific optimism, blind trust in technological progress, depersonalization of the individual, the growth of the totalitarian state.....[4]

Brought up in the hard school of the unionist scouts [4], Bernard Charbonneau persuaded his city-bound friend that the only way to get a real feel for liberty was to go out and confront Nature. And so it was that from 1930-1931 onwards Jacques Ellul used to join Charbonneau in the camping expeditions that he organized in Galicia, in the Pyrénées or in the Landes - more or less anywhere on the islands, in the mountains or in the forest - but always far from the city and the beaten track.

Charbonneau retained a taste for masculine friendships and a taste for rugged hiking trips from his days in the scouts. These student camps were the natural extension of the discussion groups that they held in his parents' sitting-room at number 6, rue du Palais Gallien. Some of the members of this group were later to become quite famous e.g. the Ecole Normale [5] educated mathematician Claude

Chevalley - a friend Arnaud Dandieu, the head of the *Ordre Nouveau* [6], Marcel Boiteux the director of the French Electricity Board, the professor of mathematics Yves Hébert, Pierre Germain the head of personnel in the Ministry of the Interior, and the Nobel prize winning physicist Alfred Kastler.

Bernard Charbonneau denied having, in any way whatsoever, wanted to imitate the young Germans of the *Wandervögel* who were in revolt against bourgeois order. He had set up these camps completely unaware of the activities of the *Jugendbewegung*. "What really drove me was the desire that any child has to get away from the constraints of the city, to find a place in which to be free, with no walls and where nothing is forbidden."

This need to find an unspoiled nature is nothing more than the corollary of a phenomenon, not discovered in the pages of a book, but observed empirically, that of the growing hold of scientific and technological organization on modern society. Or more simply, when he observed the streets that had been the setting of his childhood games being inexorably invaded by ever more cars he became acutely aware of the danger technological progress posed to his liberty.

He read Aldous Huxley's *Brave New World* (published in 1932) with enthusiasm. This book, though not the inspiration of his ideas, certainly confirmed his intuitions. But rather than chasing up idiocycrasies, however revealing they may be, let us turn to the established intellectual filiations.

During the many and heated discussions that Ellul had with Charbonneau three names cropped up again and again and who were constant guiding lights throughout Ellul's elaboration of his lifework. The first time he had come across Karl Marx was during an economics lecture course in 1929-1930 at university. Marx's criticism of capitalism provided Ellul with an explanation for his own father's unemployment. Having read *das Kapital* he was extremely disappointed when he actually met some communist workers to find that they were much more concerned with toeing the party line than with hermeneutic Marxism.

This was to leave him with a keen intellectual frustration that held him back from actually joining a political party, something he never did in fact [7]. Stalin's purges, illustrated by the first trials in Moscow in 1934-1935 were to distance him permanently. Even though he broke with communism this did not prevent him from continuing his study of Marxist thought or more importantly from teaching it later at the university.

Jacques Ellul recalled having come across Sören Kierkegaard when he was seventeen. "Thanks to him I understood that I knew nothing of real despair [8]."

Human existence considered and experienced as a permanent tension between two irreducible poles, the individual as a unique being - awareness of existential categories under the ever vigilent eye of God made man who is at all times the "Complete-Other"-, embracing faith as the only escape from the absurd, the principle of non-conformity to the world, criticism of a Church having betrayed the original message of Christ, the defense of the *individual* against Authority, these are but a few of the Danish philosopher's ideas that our French theologian addressed.

The relationship between the two is so obvious that one could call Ellul not merely Kierkegaard's spiritual heir but his kindred spirit [9]

Introduction

Whenever Charbonneau talks about his friend's works nowadays he does so in characteristically Kiekegaardian tones : "Man is free because he is placed before a contradiction that he must resolve. We live in a conflictual, incomplete, irrational world and it is precisely up to us to establish a little order even though this is difficult and provisional. The most important thing for Ellul and myself lies in the awareness of the fundamental existential contradiction between man's belonging to matter, the earth, to life, and the drive to extricate ourselves from the glebe in order to think, to add a certain order to something that in itself has no meaning. Man finds that meaning by exercising his own free-will [10]."

According to Jacques Ellul, who throughout his whole life never missed an opportunity to explain how he was completely hermetic to philosophy, "the father of existentialism" should not be considered as a philosopher. Indeed the fact that the author of *"La maladie à la Mort"* considered that philosophy belongs to the "aesthetic stage" should not be overlooked. So Kierkegaard is not an *existential philosopher* : "He situates his approach at the interface between concrete existence and life's possibilities. What in fact he reveals is his experience of suffering and love [11]."

Even though Marx and Kierkegaard are the only two authors that he claims to have read completely - with the same anarchist perspective - there is a third author, discovered at the same period for whom he explicitly claims affiliation. Jacques Ellul held the Protestant dogmatician Karl Barth (1886-1968), another brilliant dialectician, to be the greatest theologian of the twentieth century [12]. Barth, in the direct line of Kierkegaard, who considered obedience to God the sole source of bliss, enabled the young convert to think dialectically about the obedience of the free man to the free God.

The shocking revelation that the Biblical God's freedom involves not removing man's free-will. God is incognito - secret - but always there. God is transcendant but also intervenes at selected moments in History, leaving his creature free to live his destiny. God is the Almighty but speaks to man through non-almighty channels. God is the Father, the Complete-Other. God is Love but God is Justice.

Briefly, Barth's thinking enabled Jacques Ellul to avoid the *"either-or"* dilemma of the non-believers, and helped him handle the *"already"* and the "not yet", in other words the promise and its fulfilment. But above all this Swiss theologian enabled Ellul to understand the central idea of the Biblical message essentially formulated in dialectic terms : the free determination of man in the free decision of God.

At the very beginning of the thirties Ellul found himself the heir to three sources of inspiration ; Marx, Kierkegaard and Barth. The sources of inspiration for Charbonneau were much more eclectic. Moreover he claimed that his personal experience was all-embracing and he was wary of all philosophical systems.

Jacques Ellul always maintained that it was very difficult to find out what Charbonneau had or had not read. For his part Charbonneau decribed his friend as "a monster of culture whose vice is reading" just as he himself would indulge in fishing or gardening [13].

In the discussions they had as students Charbonneau, who today would deny ever having learned a thing from reading books [14], would nevertheless mention quite a few authors who would, to a greater or a lesser degree, influence Ellul's positions later on.

The thought of Tocqueville is too well-known for it to be necessary to enlarge upon here, but at nearly a century after the very successful work *Democracy in America* appeared it had strangely gone out of fashion. Nevertheless Charbonneau was to draw from it at that time for part of his criticism of western political regimes, which he was to expose after the war in a book entitled *L'Etat* [15].

To quote but a few of the theses shared by the two men : genuine democracy requires moral virtues in the population, a centralized power can rule by oppression in the name of the popular will, a liberal constitution is inapt for the protection of rights and freedoms if it condones administrative despotism, an obsession for well-being is the mother of servitude, excessive equality may well lead men to lose their taste for it.

The writing of Walter Rathenau (1867-1922) is even less well known and what is more important decidely more ambiguous [16]. We find the same mistrust towards egalitarian Utopia and the headlong race for material wealth, but this was mixed in with a very woolly theory concerning the "Popular State" which had very marked nationalist undercurrents (even discretely racist at times and outright misogynistic), in complete opposition with the positions adopted by Charbonneau.

What seems to have appealed to him in these interwoven and contradictory theses presented in a style where lyricism vies with pomposity, is the idea according to which "science should give up the right to define what the goals are to be". The distinction between truth and reality, the primacy of faith over intellectual demonstration, the requirement of personal responsibility were all topics that Ellul was to address at a later period [17].

But that is not what is essential. If Rathenau did end up behaving as a partisan for progress, he sized up the universality of the technological phenomenon thanks to his general notion of "mechanization" [18]. Charbonneau was grateful to him for having understood that the 1914-1918 war was not an ordinary war, but rather a complete upheaval of world civilization which would make modern man enter - in an entirely irreversible fashion- into a new organization which would be radically different from past systems.

In other terms, although Ellul and Charbonneau shared the overall diagnosis proposed by the author of *Où va le monde ?* their answers were the exact opposite of his. The same was the case for Oswald Spengler (1880-1936) who, in 1931, described technology as "life tactics", as a sort of interested behaviour designed to achieve certain goals and not as a set of instruments [19]. Ellul and Charbonneau did not remain insensitive to his attack on Faust-like science, of the new technological religion, of the standardized life and the ideology of progress.

They went along with Spengler's thesis according to which man having pitted himself against nature, finds that it is now his turn to be threatened by the machine which rises up against him. Are they not themselves living examples of some of his pronouncements ?

Introduction

"Faustian thinking begins to feel the affects of the nausea of the machines. Lassitude spreads, a sort of pacifism takes over in the struggle against Nature. Men go back to simpler life-styles, closer to Nature (...). They begin to find the big cities odious and they begin to want to escape from the crushing effect of soul-less events, the rigid and chilly climate of technological organization [20]."

In everything else Ellul, the Christian, and Charbonneau, the humanist, are at odds with the author of *The Decline of the West*. They were also at odds with the whole of the "national-Bolshevik" current in Germany between the two world wars, symbolized by Ernst Jünger [21].

With Ernst Von Salomon's *The Reprobates* [22], which he read as soon as it came out in France in 1931, Bernard Charbonneau was able to gauge all that separated his criticism of modern society from the whole of the "conservative revolutionary" movement. The account of this ultra-nationalist officer, an accomplice to the murder of Walter Rathenau, conveys perfectly the cult of violence that is inherent in all fascistic movements, this craze for action for action's sake inevitably leads to a passion for nothingness.

Ellul was similarly to refute any intellectual affiliation to Martin Heidegger, whom he knew to be a Nazi activist [23] as early as 1934. Not only was Ellul to believe - rightly or wrongly - that someone who made such gross errors of judgement in political thinking could be of no avail to him in his search for an understanding of the world in which we live. He also held against the author of *Being and Time* the fact that he expressed himself in a language that was far too abstract.

Jacques Ellul kept his distance from Heidegger's work, for this reason, approaching it only very indirectly through certain writings of Paul Ricoeur. For those who, in good faith, believe that they can skip Ellul's theories supposing them to be carbon copies of Heidegger's or of the theoreticians of the Frankfurt School [24], we will simply point out here - without entering into any detail - than not only had the author of *La Technique ou l'enjeu du siècle* not read the former but that he diverges on a good many points from the latter [25].

On the other hand, without finding the mark of any Heidegger influence, in the mid-thirties, Ellul and Charbonneau were already of the mind that politics was not at the "heart of things", or to talk like Dominique Janicaud [26] that the "major current of power flows less and less from politics" but more and more by techno-scientific inductors, joining the author of *Qu'est-ce que la métaphysique ?* on that.

Nevertheless it should be pointed out that unlike all the "*völkisch*" ideology spread about by numerous German essayists in the inter-war period, what they have to say bears no trace of idealization of peasantry, praise of belonging to the soil, pre-eminence of Nature, and even less trace of irrationality of anti-intellectualism.

"That is precisely what distinguished Ellul from all the totalitarians, pantheists and naturists of the day. My big idea was - though it was completely misunderstood by the ecologists - that progress is not a threat to Nature but to Liberty [27]." And for Bernard Charbonneau to explain today that all his analysis of technico-scientific rationality is based on reason. "I base myself on actual conscious experience, expressed by language and acknowledged by reason."

One of their ambitions was to bring the criticism of progress out of the mists of pastoral literature, symbolized particularly by Jean Giono. Whereas writers dominated the intellectual stage, they prefered sociological processes. "We had to get away from the disturbing gloom of the rightwing totalitarianism," recalls Charbonneau [28], "but also from the emptiness, the inoffensive-type, relaxing, irrational and compensatory wish for nature as expressed in the literature of that period."

Having more or less situated Ellul in the preceding paragraphs, it is still difficult to date with certainty the moment when Ellul and Charbonneau discovered Proudhon, Bakunin, Werner Sombart, Max Weber, Nicolas Berdiaeff, Robert Aron and Arnaud Dandieu, but it is certain that their entry into the nebulous personalist sphere was preceded by a solid theoretical grounding and a sharp awareness of the crisis facing civilization, which according to them had been spawned by the scientific and technological *revolution*.

Far from being mere mouth-pieces for, or provincial clones of, the non-conformist intellectuals up in the capital, Ellul and Charbonneau were to kindle a "Gascon" strain to the personalist movement. Just how original this was is only now becoming acknowledged by present day historians [29]. Without wishing to add to the controversy caused by Zeev Sternhell's book [30], which described the non-conformist movement of the thirties as a sort of template for pro-fascist culture, we can safely say that the "Bordeaux group", which was driven by ideals of liberty, humanism and Christianity deserved no such charges levelled against it.

"Christianity is not a revolution in itself but at the origin of all revolution", a statement appearing in March 1933 in *Esprit* from the pen of Alexander Marc : one of the main organizers of *Ordre Nouveau*. A point of view that Ellul clearly shared, and to a lesser extent Charbonneau, looking for a *third way* between spiritualism and materialism, between individualism and collective tyranny, between the liberal State and a totalitarian State.

When at about this time the two Bordelais were to go up to Paris to meet Emmanuel Mounier, the review *Esprit* which the latter had founded in 1932 had no more than six hundred subscribers and a circulation of two thousand for each issue. Jean-Louis Loubet del Bayle [31] was right when he described these two rebellious middle-class young men in revolt against the *established disorder* as "a minority within an aging society". Our two Gascons would always remain at the fringe of this minority movement.

Michel Winock [32] has clearly shown how *Esprit* emerged as a movement caused by the conjunction of three crises : a society traumatized by the war and the economic depression, a labour movement torn asunder by the October revolution, a Catholic environment badly integrated into civil society. This state of affairs throws light on the origins of the other two poles of personalism represented by *Ordre Nouveau* and the *Jeune Droite* [33].

These *Années tournantes* [34] (The Watershed Years) were also preceded by the reappearance of the ultra-rightwing leagues - particularly through the *Jeunesses Patriotes* [35] (the Patriotic Youth) which so worried Ellul already when he was a lycée student - and a certain number of political-financial scandals only served to further fuel a climate already propititious to antiparliamentarianism and discredit of the political class.

If one is to question the role of the Great War in the tremendous unrest felt by the young generation, if one had been able to discuss the truly innovatory nature of the period of intellectual effervescence, there is no doubt that Ellul and Charbonneau, "aware of living in unprecedented times [36]", fit perfectly into that *No generation* [37] of which they were both actors and witnesses.

Being neither individualists, nor collectivists, nor identifying with the figures of individualistic liberalism nor with the "political soldiers [38]" of the totalitarian movements, their quest was for an anti-capitalistic, anti-fascist but non-communist movement. Our two Bordelais found the personalist movement had a doctrine which corresponded globally to what they themselves were hoping for, all the more so that it was developing before their eyes and that they had every intention of bringing it their contribution.

Back in Bordeaux, Charbonneau decided to affiliate his small discussion group [39], which adopted this name officially at the beginning of 1934. In the June issue of the review the first account of their activities appeared in the "Friends of *Esprit* column", written in a telegraphic style and highly instructive for all that [40].

"Bordeaux : Lengthy study of our two surveys. Next tackled the federal issue in the following vein : "Keep man in contact with his neighbours, with a world in which real life is the only source of creation, without forgetting shared higher realities for all that, which should be the very principle of respect for all diversity, and also the necessity of maintaining sufficient exchanges between these seats of autonomous life to fuel their existence." Suggested that group members hold regional meetings, particularly during the holidays, "as the opportunity presents itself."

The Friends column in the December issue announced that "the Bordeaux group" had presented the Paris editorial staff with the year's work on federalism and the new law [41], and that it had held two conferences on *Esprit*.. We also learn that the Bordelais had invited other groups to join forces with them to buy a printing press and that they encouraged members living in the same region to go camping together rather than hold their usual annual congress.

The space devoted to the activities of the Bordeaux group in the "friends column" in the January 1935 issue was much more detailed than that of the other cities [42]. We learn that the Bordeaux personalists [43] had organized themselves into an "action group" and "an education group" to present the questions dealt with by the action group to a wider public.

They rotated each week. The group seemed to want to experience, with a singular intensity, the daily and "earthy" nature of the revolution. It undertook a series of awareness-raising sessions on the "unreality of the present-day world", all the phoney romanticism which slips into a certain conception of the home-land, politics, the cult of the hero and of famous people, in the illusions of liberties, all sorts of escapism.

"Study the technique of spiritual means on : the press, money, the crowd, "friends and aquaintances". Always insist that the spiritual revolution is more material, more tangible than all others. Insist also on the necessity of inter-group regional meetings and lateral liaising between groups."

Even though the riots of the 6th Febuary 1934 were to further reinforce Ellul's anti-fascist feelings, he did not let himself get trapped in a bipolar logic and reduce his struggle to the political plane alone. In "Personalism, instant revolution", the opening article in the first issue of the *Journal du Groupe de Bordeaux des Amis d'Esprit* [44], apart from a few digs at Colonel de La Rocque's Croix-de-feu [45], Jacques Ellul exposed a series of theses which he would expand and research throughout the rest of his life : nowadays men are no longer gathered in "communities" of individuals capable of making personal judgements but are simply a "crowd" conditioned by propaganda, the liberating Christianity of early times has moulted away into the opposite, the real revolution should begin "within each individual", this revolution carried out on oneself and with others should be permanent, the "person" is invincible to scientific classification, to change regime you must first "begin by changing people's lives", in modern society the true combat is above all a spiritual one and political differences are secondary......

From this time onwards the Bordeaux group was no longer hitting it off with the Paris editorial board, as can be witnessed in this extract from the unpublished *Carnets* (Notebooks) of Mounier of the 9th of March 1935 : "This little handful of Protestants round Charbonneau who share visions of revolution and disorder in the language of small town gossip and parochial ideas. Somewhat Jansenist, though solid, peasant-like, hard-working (they pass around a journal that they have cyclo-styled themselves). They have more or less sworne themselves to celibacy to be better able to carry out the spiritual revolution : all that rather boyish but very ardent [46]."

As far as they were concerned, Ellul and Charbonneau criticized Mounier for his centralizing authoritarianism, his intellectual Paris bias and his hard-nosed Catholicism, and even though they continued to express their ideas through *Esprit* [47], they were nevertheless to build up contacts with Denis de Rougement and Alexander Marc, the people running *Ordre Nouveau* with whom they had a similar orientation [48] on many points.

Not only were Ellul and Charbonneau impressed by the pertinence of the analyses of the duo Aron/Dandieu [49], the theoretical basis of the rival review, but they were also to find a criticism of *mechanized society* as well as similar sensitivity on matters of liberty and federalism to their own. Unfortunately for them, the anti-state control stance of *Ordre Nouveau* [50], was curiously tempered with notions of economic planning, very much in vogue at the time and already presented in the *Esprit* programme.

Furthermore, in spite of their announced intentions, the community dimension so essential to the "Gascon" personalists was almost practically inexistent in *Ordre nouveau*. Ellul and Charbonneau were always insisting on the necessity of setting up, locally, small self-governing groups which would be federated between themselves. They would function as counter-societies, these exemplary groups - the embodiment of the order to construct - were not intended for the overthrow of the regime but as evidence, here and now, of the *instant revolution*. Gradually, contagiously, this network founded at the base could spread even beyond national

Introduction

frontiers, which were bound to disappear anyway. Hence their repeated injunctions uttered in the columns of the review for the establishing of "lateral links" between the various *Esprit* groups.

To bring about the revolution, according to the "Gascons" who always advocated a "down to earth" realism, it is not enough simply to share the same ideas . it is necessary to be able to live together and on a daily basis if possible in direct contact with nature. Paradoxically in appearance, only a community of "united and isolated" men would guarantee the existence of an authentic inner life denied by the technological civilization.

As from October 1935, Ellul and Charbonneau were to give a series of lectures in Bordeaux, Pau and Bayonne, on the necessity of creating a personalist society to resist the "inevitabilities facing us in the presentday society" : war, fascism, "concentration" in all its forms (economic, financial, political and demographic) made possible by means of "technology". [51] In particular they expose their notion of "social sin", committed by those who accept to give up on their vocation for liberty and conform to social pressures. They indulge in the exegesis of all the commonplace statements bandied about by the media.

Reporting on the activities of the Pau personalists in December 1936, and in particular during a visit by Ellul, the critic Roger Breuil wrote the following : "We are torn between two tendencies *Esprit* (pretty imperious), *Ordre nouveau* (rigorous) and Charbonnist (not always very well thought out in their constructive part)". This led the Canadian historian Christian Roy [52] to write that : "The distinctive brand of personalism advocated by Charbonneau and Ellul was clearly acknowledged".

Whether Mounier liked it or not, the "Gascons" were not destined to celibacy since Jacques Ellul met Yvette Lensvelt at the Law School and was to marry her in 1937. Bernard Charbonneau, for his part, met the woman who was to become his wife, a certain Henriette Daudin, German specialist and daughter of a communist member of the Faculty.

After succeeding in the History-Geography *agrégation* exam - to be recruited into the teaching profession, Charbonneau settled in Bayonne but maintained close links with the Bordeaux group. Meanwhile Ellul was finishing off his doctorate in law, giving private classes to pay for his studies, animating various Protestant youth clubs and associations, working with Charbonneau on the composition of a text which was to put in condensed form the essential ideas of their present and future work. [53]

These *Directives for a personalist manifesto* turn around a thiry-three point diagnosis entitled *The origin of our revolt* followed by fifty propositions grouped under the heading *Direction for the construction of a personalist society*. This manifesto given over to the Ellul-Charbonneau thesis of the powerlessness of politics in the face of the supremacy of technology which affects the capitalist, fascist and communist regimes in the same way.

It describes a phenomenon of generalized proletization in a world where man is no longer the measure of all things. Only a revolution could remedy this degradation, for all attempts at reform would only end up reinforcing the alienating structures. The revolution which the personalists would carry out is neither political nor moral. "Revolution of civilization", must be carried out in different ways from those taken by the fascists and the communists, otherwise they would be doomed to failure. It would have to go via the establishment of a "personalist society" within the global society.

While awaiting the self-destruction of the present society, this counter-society would be preparing the executives of tomorrow. Its members would therefore have to limit their participation in the technological society. For the time being, it was a matter of managing to achieve a pragmatic and dogmatic doctrinal formation. This doctrine would make action possible, more precisely a reaction towards the world, a new mentality which would inspire a new life-style.

Their life-style would be the outward sign of their active commitment. Elective communities would then be set up to replace the city. Within these small volunteer groups, man would feel wholly himself with roots somewhere real. In this "city scaled to man", real politics, based on direct communication between the rulers and the ruled, would be conducted in the open. Countries would be divided into regions with a central State having limited authority.

Hence only federalism would have the flexibility to co-ordinate these autonomous units. "Security would come from the reduction of the effective power of the States". A federally organized society would have the effect of limiting the extent of economic crises by controlling technology. Having a controlled technology, at the service of man, would facilitate the reduction of working time. The private economic sector would be reserved for the production of quality products, products essential for subsistence would be made by the public sector. The struggle against the power of Money in modern society would be achieved by abolishing all usury, and profits would be abolished.

As far as bourgeois family structures were concerned, there would be no reason to retain them. Only a re-newed family community would find its place in the personalist society, without actually forming its basis. The question of property could be resolved by using the formula : "One only has what one possesses [54]." Property should correspond to what is actually used or enjoyed. Inheritance would be tolerated in as far as it evidences a family continuity, with the exclusion of the transmission of money, position or privilege.

The modern law, having become a simple set of technical rules and regulations, would revive the two essential elements of Law : the meaning of justice and the reality of life. A preponderant place would be given to custom, under the control of a judge, this would lead to the appearance of a "living law".

Because of its disasterous influence, advertizing would be scrutinized by the government. The gossip press would disappear leaving the place to local papers and wall-news. There would be no programme concerning living art, the best expression of man, nor would it be locked up in a museum. "We will see the sign that a real revolution has taken place when we see a new art emerging from within art and without theories to explain it."

This total revolution, conducted both against poverty and against wealth in the framework of an *ascetic civil society*, would then produce a balanced society on both the material and the spiritual level.

Introduction

From 1937, differences between the Bordeaux group and the editorial board of *Esprit* in Paris were to widen. Emmanuel Mounier even went so far as to call Charbonneau a "bad-tempered little schoolboy" in a letter which Charbonneau tore up in a fit of anger. Fed up with waiting for this intellectual review to turn into a truly revolutionary movement, the two Gascons resigned from *Esprit*, without giving up on their project for all that.

When Mounier died, Jacques Ellul spoke at length about their differences which he felt were linked to a deep theological difference : "He was unable to give up the idea of man being able to decide almost freely, to choose the use (of technology, State or money) and, demiurge, at each instant always able to dominate external forces (......), he was unable to accept what he termed my *"prophetism"* or my *"catastrophism"* [55]."

Ellul was separated from his friend Charbonneau first when he went as a senior lecture in Montpellier before his nomination in Strasbourg in 1938 and then for a while by the war. When the students and staff of Strasbourg University withdrew to Clermont-Ferrand, Jacques Ellul - denounced by one of his students for having uttered allegedly subversive ideas - was removed from his post on the grounds that he was the child of an alien. Furthermore his father was arrested and imprisoned by the Germans only a short time after that incident.

During the summer of 1940, Ellul and his wife were able to return to the outskirts of Bordeaux before settling in the Entre-deux-Mers region. In the little village of Martres, in the Gironde, Ellul turned himself into a farmworker in order to feed his family. At the same time as he was revising for the *agrégation* [56] exam in Roman law and history of law, which he succeeded in 1943, he was working with the Resistance but he never used arms. Ellul passed on information to the *maquis* or underground, hid escaping prisoners and Jewish friends, managing to get them forged papers and helping them to get over into the French free-zone. Thanks to the benevolent cover of the *assesseur du doyen* [57] (deputy dean), he was able to give a few clandestine classes at the Bordeaux Law School which was filled with mainly Pétainist supporters.

At the Liberation Ellul, as secretary general - for the Bordeaux region - of the *Mouvement de libération nationale* [58], sat on several collaborationist trials and did whatever was in his power, with the backing of the future *Préfet* Gabriel Delaunay, to prevent the purge getting out of hand and going too far.

At the request of the *commissaire de la République* [59], Gaston Cusin, Ellul joined the provisional interim municipal council of Bordeaux. This council was set up by the commissaire in order to ensure the interim between the collaborationist and the forthcoming freely elected municipal council. It was presided by the Socialist Fernand Audeguil. This council sat from the 31st of October 1944 to the 25th of April 1945 [60]. From that six-month experience Ellul drew the conclusion that representatives are forever at the mercy of the "bureaux" and that politics is powerless up against bureaucracy. He refused to be included on the Socialist list at the municipal elections in spring 1945. He did however play a very active part in the general elections - both legislative and referendum - on the 21st of October 1945. He was number three on the list of the *Union démocratique et socialiste de la Résistance (UDSR)*. In the Gironde this list was under the official patronage of two internal Resistance organizations the *Mouvement de Libération Nationale (MLN)* and the *Organisation Civile et Militaire (OCM)*. Ellul, the university professor, who in addition stood for secretary general of the MLN took his candidacy very seriously and participated actively in the election campaign. Judging from the police report of the period he conducted several public meetings in Pessac, Arcachon, Bègles, Talence and Bordeaux to defend his party's programme.

In all his campaign speeches he presented himself as new arrival on the political scene. He called for genuine "revolution" in France. According to him, the people would only be able to express their sovereignty with the advent of a really stable government where ministers were accountable to the citizens. Ellul demanded an end to *le cumul des mandats* (the holding of more than one office at a time). He advocated the disbanding of the *Sénat* in favour of an economic upper chamber. He called for a ban on trusts and for the nationalization of all the nation's vital resources. His speech always ended with a statement of his conviction that the referendum must be answered by a double yes and that de Gaulle deserved support.

Unfortunately the outcome of these elections did not match the effort that had been put into them. The ballot-box dealt a cruel verdict. The UDSR list scored about 18,000 votes in the whole of the Gironde, in other terms only 4.77% of the votes cast, so obtained not a single *député*.

This defeat coupled with the rather frustrating experience Ellul had had in the city hall was to distance him for all time from the official political arena. Thus as early as 1947 he turned down the offer of Jacques Chaban Delmas to be on his list.

He also turned down the offer of an appointment as *préfet* preferring to devote his time and energy to his students at the Bordeaux Law School and at the Political Studies Institute in Bordeaux, and to writing his life work which was to include a thousand articles, fifty books translated into twelve different languages. In addition to his historical writing, in particular his five volume *Histoire des Institutions*, which was to be a set-work for several generations of law students, Jacques Ellul admitted that his books on sociology and theology were written in deliberately different registers but insisted that there was nevertheless a close correspondence between the two.

La Technique ou l'enjeu du siècle, the first book in a trilogy devoted to a criticism of technological society, came out in France in 1954 thanks to the support of his colleague Maurice Duverger. Aldous Huxley came across this work and recommended it to the president of the University in Santa Barbara. As a result of this ten years later Ellul had a good and lasting reputation in the United States.

His theology writing really took off in 1948 with the publication of *Présence au monde moderne* and ended in 1987 with *La Raison d'être*, his meditation on the Book of Ecclesiastes [61]. One of the indirect consequences of the success of *The Technological Society* was that people at the other side of the Atlantic also wanted to read his "religious" books which indeed enjoyed quite a wide circulation, to such an extent that some of them appeared in America before they even found an editor in France.

Having decided to turn his back on playing an active part in political life at the beginning of the fourth Republic, Ellul nevertheless continued to incarnate his

Introduction

notion of what a Christian's place was in the world [62], as far removed from the fundamentalists, as the theologians of liberation. Invested with a prophetic mission, the believer, by his thought and by his action - completely cut off from all the social conformisms - brings in the power of eschatology. This faith in the glorious return of Jesus Christ places the Christian in a revolutionary situation and enables him to face up to all technological dictatorship.

From the early post-war period Jacques Ellul held a position of national responsibility at the head of the Reformed Church, which did not prevent him from remaining a marginal within the Protestant community, often he was better thought of by Jews and Catholics than by his co-religionists.

His involvement in the present age fueled his writing. He rekindled the tradition of camps in the mountains, but this time with small groups of students whom he trained in the critical analysis of all the manifestations of modern society, be they political, cultural, social or artistic.

From 1958 to 1977, Ellul was the president of a juvenile deliquency prevention club as well as playing a very active part in the ecological struggle, particularly within the Committee for the protection of the Aquitaine coast where he met his old friend Charbonneau again. Always faithful to their boyhood maxim : "Think globally, act locally", the two men never gave up on their project to change society from outside the political party structures.

Right to the end of his life, Jacques Ellul continued to personify the Christian and anarchistic values he had always advocated, with a rare constance for a French intellectual. Indifferent to fashions, overlooked by the television stations, this free spirit never hesitated to swim against the tide to conserve his integrity.

His work was ostracised for a long time, there is still a great deal to be discovered. And even so Ellul the pioneer of ecology thought of *Le Contrat Naturel* before Michel Serres. As a specialist on propaganda he discovered that there was no such thing as *public opinion* before Pierre Bourdieu. With his exegesis of the common place, he anticipated Roland Barthes' *Mythologies*. He denounced the *self-hatred* of Third World supporters and the betrayal of the West before Pascal Bruckner. His ideas enabled Ivan Illich to think up the notions of *thresholds* of development and of *convivial austerity*. It's too bad that of all these authors only the last on the list was to acknowledge his indebtedness to Ellul which he did most warmly as it turns out.

Because he painted a rather somber picture of the technological society with man the plaything of the propaganda machine, state oppression and political illusion, Ellul has often been accused of describing a world in ruins. However hope and freedom were at the heart of all his work, as will become clear from a perusal of the following pages in the company of the man himself.

---

[1] "Qui êtes-vous ?" (Who are you ?), La Manufacture.
[2] Interview with Bernard Charbonneau, 24th July, 1993.
[3] Bernard Charbonneau, historian and geographer, was born on the 28th of November 1910 in Bordeaux and died on the 28th of April 1996 in the Pyrénées, where he had chosen to settle

down far from the Parisian media whirl. Jacques Ellul always considered him to be one of the unacknowledged geniuses of his time.

[4] The Fédération des Eclaireurs unionistes de France, founded in 1921, is the Protestant scout movement in France.

[5] The Ecole Normale Supérieure, rue d'Ulm in Paris. This highly prestigious seat of higher learning known familiarly as "Normal'Sup" is the prototype of the *Grande Ecole*. It was founded in 1794. Among its long list of famous alumni are such intellectuals as Jean-Paul Sartre and Raymond Aron.

[6] This was a *personalist* review, set up in the thirties and animated by the federalist Alexandre Marc and the Protestant Denis de Rougemont. Should NOT be confused with an extreme rightwing movement, of the same name, that appeared in Paris in 1970 and was dissolved in 1973 as a result of a series of ugly clashed brought about by the group's xenophobic message.

[7] William H. Vanderburg, *Perspectives on Our age. Jacques Ellul speaks on his life and work*, Canadian Broadcasting Corporation, Toronto, 1981, p.6, and discussions with Ellul subsequent to an article in the *Figaro* on the 6th of August, 1992.

[8] Discussion with Jacques Ellul on the 14th of October, 1987.

[9] Vernard Eller, "Ellul and Kierkegaard : closer than brothers" in *Jacques Ellul : Interpretive Essays*, Christians and Van Hook, Universirty of Illinois Press, Chicago, 1981, pp. 52-66.

[10] Discussion with Bernard Charbonneau, 24th of July, 1993.

[11] Jacques Ellul and Didier Nordon, *L'Homme à lui-même*, Paris, Editions du Félin, 1992, p. 26.

[12] Jacques Ellul, *Anarchie et christianisme*, Lyon, Atelier de création lbertaire, 1988, p. 13.

[13] Discussion with B.C. and J.E.

[14] Discussion with Bernard Charbonneau, 24th July, 1993.

[15] This work was completed in 1949, and published in roneo in 1951 and re-edited by Economica in 1987.

[16] Walter Rathenau, upper-middle class well-educated of Jewish origin, was trained as an engineer and the son of the founder of AEG, one of the major electricity trusts, he was to succeed his father in that position. He was both a man of reflexion and a man of action. He was a nationalist and a pacifist, leader of the German Democratic Party, he was one of the founders of the Weimar Republic. Minister of Reconstruction in1921, then minister of Foreign Affairs. He was assasinated on June 24, 1922 by some extreme-right-wing officers for having been in favour of the Germano-Soviet rapprochement established by the Treaty of Rapallo.

[17] Ellul quotes this book in the bibliography of *The Technological Society*.

[18] *De la mécanique de l'esprit* was published as early as 1913.

[19] Oswald Spengler, 1931 (*Der Mensch und die Technik*), *L'Homme et la technique*, Paris, Gallimard, 1969, p.44.

[20] *Ibid., p.167.*

[21] On the ideological imbroglio that existed at that time *cf.* Peter Gay, 1968, *Le Suicide d'une République (Weimar Culture)*, Paris, Calmann-Lévy, 1993, Pierre Bourdieu, *L'Ontologie politique de Martin Heidegger*, Paris, Minuit, 1988, and Jean-Michel Palmier, "Heidegger et le national-socialisme" in *Cahier de l'Herne*, 1983.

[22] *Les Réprouvés(Die Geächteten)*, Paris, Plon (collection "Feux croisés" edited by Gabriel Marcel), 1931.

[23] Interview with Jacques Ellul, 15 January, 1988. Contrary to the debate surrounding the "discovery" of Heidegger's Nazi commitment which recurs roughly every ten years, this fact

Introduction

was well established before the war as evidenced by the following extract from an article written by José Bergamin, published in April 1937 in *Esprit* : "Why Being rather than Nothingness ?" asks the metaphysist of agonished and agonizing fascism, of German national-socialism, the philosopher of Nothingness, Heidegger", p.103.

[24] He only came across the Frankfurt School (if fact only two of the : Adorno and Habermas), at the beginning of the sixties. Hence a long time after he had written his major work on technology.

[25] For a comparison of these two, *cf.* Maurice Weyembergh, *Entre politique et technique,* Paris, Vrin, 1991, and "Le prophète et le penseur" in *Sur Jacques Ellul,* published under the direction of Patrick Troude-Chastenet, Bordeaux, L'Esprit du Temps/PUF, 1994.

[26] *La Puissance du rationnel,* Paris, Gallimard, 1985, p.83.

[27] Interview with Bernard Charbonneau, 24, July 1993.

[28] Interview with Bernard Charbonneau, 24, July, 1993.

[29] *Cf* the excellent article on this point by Christian Roy, "On the origins of political ecology :The "Gascon" personalism of Bernard Charbonneau and Jacques Ellul", *Canadian Journal of History, XXVII, April/1992, pp. 67-100.*

[30] *Ni droite ni gauche. L'idéologie fasciste en France,* Paris, Seuil, 1983.

[31] *Les Non-conformistes des années trente. Une tentative de renouvellement de la pensée politique française,* Paris, Seuil, 1969, p.28.

[32] *Histoire politique de la revue "Esprit".* 1930-1950, Paris, Seuil, 1975.

[33] Regrouped around Thierry Maulnier, Jean-Pierre Maxence and Jean de Fabrègues, these dissidents from Action Française mainly used as their mouth-piece *Réaction pour l'ordre, La Revue française* and *La Revue du siècle.* Ellul and Charbonneau had no contact with them whatsoever.

[34] The title of a book by Henri Daniel-Rops (1901-1965) published in December 1932. Historian and novelist close to the *Ordre Nouveau.*

[35] Situated halfway between the antiparliamentary league and fascist organizations, the *Jeunesses Patriotes,* was founded in 1924 by the Bonapartist député Pierre Taittinger. A paramilitary movement (recognizable by their blue raincoats and Basque berets) the *Jeunesses Patriotes* were used as a strongarm contingent by the parliamentary rightwing.

[36] Interview with Bernard Charbonneau.

[37] And who thought of themselves as such!. The publicity strip round the first issue of *Esprit* announced : "The review of the new generation." Inside on page 129 one also finds : "The origin of our accord is a shared impossibility to live."

[38] A phrase coined by Denis de Rougement (1906-1985), a Swiss Protestant of the Barth persuasion, one of the main founders of *Esprit* and *L'Ordre Nouveau,* author of *Politique de la personne* (1934), *Penser avec les mains* (1936), *L'Amour et l'Occident* (1939).

[39] According to his own confession Charbonneau had few organisational skills so he gave the title of local correspondent to the review to his friend Jean Imberti, the son of the owner of an important paint store, very well-introduced in Bordeaux circles.Ellul could not stand him, finding him an esthete and lazy into the bargain. Ellul was, moreover to take his place from the end of 1934.

[40] *Esprit,* 1st of June 1934, n°21, pp.518-519.

[41] This refers no doubt to an unpublished text of Ellul entitled "For a living law", which the bibliographer Joyce Main Hanks, author of the indispensible *Jacques Ellul : A Comprehensive Bibliography,* has kindly sent us a copy.

[42] *Esprit,* 1st January 1935, n°28, p. 700.

[43] Some fifteen or so people according to the recollections of Ellul and Charbonneau.

[44] This sixteen page typewritten bulletin(not dated) that Ellul had cyclo-styled himself, was sold for 1.50 F. The three day study camp held in the mountains which is mentioned on the last page, together with reference to an earlier pamphlet containing the programme of the meetings of the Bordeaux group, makes it possible to situate the date when it came out to between July and October 1935.

[45] At the outset this movement was simply an ex-serviceman association, but the Croix-de-feu (Cross of fire) was to become a mass movement in 1931 under the impetus of Colonel François de la Rocque. Opponents of this movement described it as "fascistic" because of their anticommunism and paramilitary marches. Nowadays historians qualify the Croix-de-feu as being "social-patriotic Christian" or "politically involved scouts".

[46] *Carnets* (Notebooks) VIII, unpublished, in Christian Roy, art. quoted p. 86.

[47] Ellul and Charbonneau were never to publish articles in *Ordre Nouveau*. Charbonneau explains today that the editorial board of *Esprit* was more open and what is more certain esoteric masonic orientations of *Ordre Nouveau* were not to his liking.

[48] *Cf.* J-L. Loubet del Bayle, "Aux origines de la pensée de Jacques Ellul ?" in *Sur Jacques Ellul, op. cit.*

[49] It is not possible to say whether Ellul had read *Le Cancer américain* (Rieder, 1931) and *La Révolution nécessaire* (Grasset, 1933) when they came out. These two books are mentioned in the bibliography of *La Technique ou l'enjeu du siècle* with incorrect references quite simply because his books had been confiscated at that time by an eminent colleague when Ellul was removed from office in 1940.

[50] In May 1933 the review was to open its first issue with an article by Daniel-Rops with the very evocate title : "The State versus man".

[51] Among the titles of these lectures we find : "The liberal perversion", "The inevitabilities of the modern world", "Moral forces", "The formation of modern cities", "Progress versus man", "The personalist technique", "Fascism, the spawn of liberalism", "Revolution for an escetic civilization, against poverty and against wealth".

[52] Art. quoted, p.80.

[53] In 1986 Jacques Ellul showed me this fifteen page type-written document dated 1935, whereas the research worker Christian Roy dates its appearance as being during the winter of 1937.

[54] The influence of Proudhon can be felt here already in the federalist theories.

[55] *Réforme*, n° 265, 15 April 1950.

[56] This examination is a national competition to recruit the professorial élite in higher education. Even since 1896 the *agrégation* for law faculties has been divided into four sections : public law, private law, economics, Roman law and history of law.

[57] The *doyen* who was elected by his peers was head of administration, teaching and research for the whole of the law school. His deputy helped him in these tasks and generally succeeded him. Thus the Pétainist Roger Bonnard was appointed Dean in 1940 and was replaced in 1944 by his deputy Henri Vizioz.

[58] Headed by Henri Frenay. Several resistance organizations merged together to form the MLN which, in 1943, was one of the two major internal Resistance organizations. Wishing to continue the struggle on the political scene the MLN rallied some 500.000 members round a labour-like programme. It is interesting to note that one its members was André Malraux. The MLN nevertheless failed to achieve its major goal that of founding a unified gathering from the Resistance which would replace the old pre-war parties. By January 1945, party activists were drifting over to the National Front which was run by the communists, or the SFIO (socialist), the *Jeune République*, the radicals or towards the *Mouvement républicain populaire* (MRP). In June 1945, a small group from the MLN founded the *Union*

démocratique et socialiste de la résistance (UDSR), a small but pivotal party which gathered Gaullists, socialists and moderates (centre right) such as the future president François Mitterrand or Eugène Claudius-Petit who was later to offer Ellul a post as *préfet*.

[59] The *commissaires de la République* were intended to replace the *préfet*s - appointed by the Vichy régime - they were to represent the State and more precisely the government of General de Gaulle.

[60] Curiously all the biographical notes concerning Ellul give the dates for his municipal experience as 1944 until 1947.

[61] Reason for being : A Meditation on Ecclesiastes. Tr. Joyce Main Hanks. Grand Rapids : Eerdmans, 1990.

[62] *Cf.* on this point Gabriel Vahanian's, "Sacré, technique et société" and Jean-Louis Seurin's, "L'interprétation de la politique à la lumière de la Bible", in *Sur Jacques Ellul, op. cit.*

CHAPTER ONE

Provincial. Minority. One book. A world without prospects. The Holy Spirit. Political power. The cold monster. Anarchy and Christianity. Reactionary. Humble words. Environmentalists. A libertarian Marx. New philosophers for the old right. Happiness. Intellectual responsibility. Pessimism and Manicheanism. Non-conformism. Non-violence. Means and ends.

Patrick CHASTENET - *You seem to be the perfect personification of the old adage, "no man is a prophet in his own country" ! In your opinion, what explains your success abroad and your belated popularity in France ? Far from Paris, no salvation ?*

Jacques ELLUL - To a large extent my success abroad was due to the fact my book on the technological society came out in America at a time when the Americans were experiencing the sort of problems I was talking about. As far as France is concerned, being provincial is always a determining factor if one wants a career as a writer or a philosopher. Several years ago a Parisian journalist came home here to interview me and asked : "But how can you be an intellectual if you live in the provinces ?" That was a very typical reaction ! Anyhow I've always been quite marginal in all the activities I have been involved in.

I had a university career but did little work in my speciality. I am a Christian, but being a Protestant I am in a minority religion and within Protestantism I belong to an even smaller minority. Naturally I've always been on the side-lines because I've always refused to join any of the mainstream political currents. Perhaps this has something to do with my character. I have the habit of always starting by criticizing all the things I like, which does not necessarily endear me to those who are close to me. Consequently I don't tend to criticize right-wing ideas or people since I have nothing in common with them, but I do criticize the left because I have friends there and a certain affinity for them. So it is obvious that I have always found myself alone and out of place.

You seem happy to play on two registers : the theological and the socio-political. In your works we find the same kind of analysis, adapted to different fields of study. This is the case, for example with "Politique de Dieu, politique des hommes" *and* "L'Illusion Politique", *published one year earlier. Is it possible to consider one aspect of your work without having to refer to the other ?*

If you were to look at one without the other there would always be something missing. If you only take the theological dimension into account, you miss the element of incarnation. If you restrict yourself to looking at the socio-political dimension, you will be constantly running up against lack of answers and narrowness. In fact, as one of my readers quite rightly pointed out, I have not actually written a wide variety of books but rather one long book in which each "individual book" constitutes a chapter. It's a gamble and a little insane to believe that there will be some readers patient enough to see how my thirty-six works [1] actually belong together.

Without God, does your work still have a meaning ?

Without God, my work would have an eminently tragic meaning. It would have driven me to taking the same way out as Romain Gary : suicide. I describe a world with no prospects but I have the conviction that God accompanies man throughout history.

You are aware that some of your readers are atheists ?

Yes, but I believe that what I have to say about Christianity is open to everyone including non-believers. By that I mean that hope is transmissible, even without reference to a given God. Hope is the link between the two sides of what I write, which communicate back and forth in a sort of dialectical exchange in which hope is both the crisis point and the solution.

You are very suspicious of spiritualists, of abstract religions. Your God was made Man because the Son of God was crucified on the cross, some people claim that an exclusive attachment to the person of Christ has made Christianity a religion of suffering and death. The Church of Rome has placed a greater importance on Christ than on the Holy Spirit. Should Christ be transcended in this day and age ?

That has always been a temptation in the different Christian movements. The kingdom of the Spirit leads only to an awareness of who Jesus Christ is and on the other hand of who God is. These are not successive kingdoms, one refers to the other. Jesus evokes God the Father, as the Holy Spirit evokes Jesus and God the Father in the Trinity. But, a tragic error in Christianity has been to see Christ as crucified and as remaining crucified. It is true, as Pascal says, that Christ is crucified until the end of time, but it must not be forgotten that in the Gospels, the crucifixion only makes sense in the resurrection. It's the resurrection that gives the crucifixion its dimension and meaning. Without the resurrection, the death of Jesus is nothing more than that of any other dissident. If we don't look beyond what happened at the Passion, the message of sorrow and despair this gives is not at all in keeping with the message of the Gospels : good news !

Why does the Holy Ghost have to intervene ?

Actually it is to make us reason in reverse. In the revelation, we must start at the end in order to understand the beginning. This is precisely what the Holy Spirit makes us do : see the cross through the resurrection, similarly, to see man's

Chapter 1

sins through forgiveness. Condemnation through grace. It's because God forgives us that we are able to realize the extent to which we have sinned ; while the natural way for man to proceed would be to sin and then to ask God's forgiveness. For me, this is therefore entirely open and entirely liberating. It is a heresy to preach about sins and condemnation before preaching about of freedom and forgiveness.

Concerning the nature of political power, are your doubts founded on a Protestant interpretation of the Bible or rather on your personal experience of the Liberation ?

Very clearly from my personal experience. Prior to the Liberation there had already been a succession of deceptions. We had hopes at the time of the Spanish civil war... Those of us who were on the side of the Republicans witnessed the failure of the revolution ; in 1936 the revolution failed ; in 1944 I was one of those who, wrongly, hoped that we would go from resistance to revolution. Three set-backs of that magnitude, believe me, are harder to bear than '68 ! Later on my very brief experience in public life after the Liberation proved to be unsuccessful, I had the impression that the way into politics was completely blocked. There were all sorts of intrigues and plots going on, in short, always the same old story... Hence it's not at all my Calvinist interpretation of the Bible which caused me to withdraw, it was my personal experience which lead me to that conclusion.

You denounce any idolization of the State. All through your writing there is an obvious basic mistrust of the State. Some right-wingers must warm to your anti-governmentalism whereas the state socialists, almost the entire French left, are hostile to this standpoint. Where does this suspicion of the State, which you have nurtured since your youth, come from ?

Looking back at the French state between 1930 and 1933, it seemed civil and well-intentioned. Nevertheless we sensed all the underlying dangers. A certain number of us experienced a feeling of dread at the increased power of the State. It was as if Evil was attacking and taking control of society. Obviously this impression was reinforced by the fascist and Nazi experience and by the transformation of the federal Bolshevik state - the Soviets - into a centralised and bureaucratic state. This is why we really had the feeling that the State was everything Nietzsche had said it was : "The coldest of cold monsters". I realized that the State has become even more abstract as a result of its administrative apparatus. At least you know who the enemy is when one person has the power.

Is it important to be able to identify the enemy ?

In the modern State, the much vaunted decision making centres are so numerous and so evanescent that one is completely powerless against them. That is why I have always felt we should fight against the administrative State on one the hand and for power to be given back to the grass roots.

Jacques Ellul

Is there no leader in your analysis ? Is there a sort of spontaneous coordination ?

Hitler's death did not put an end to the concentration camps nor to the torture. Hitler had served to crystallize the aspirations of a society at a particular moment in time. It is for this reason that even if a leader exists, he does not interest me for he is incidental. What interests me, is the mechanism of the process.

The mistakes, the dead ends, and in some cases the crimes of today's left have provoked a sort of tacit compromise between the liberals and the anarchistics. Do you see yourself as what might be called a "liberal-libertarian" ?

Liberal, I am not. I don't believe in liberty in itself. I don't believe it is possible to find the necessary institutions with which to instill liberty. I'm pretty close to being a libertarian, but libertarian with a great difference : my anarchist friends believe that a libertarian society is possible whereas I believe it is quite impossible. However in the present situation, it's the only vehicle with which to fight against an authority which is extending itself into all sectors of society. In other words, we should be willing to give back a certain decision-making power to the most diverse and multiple groups, and try to avoid the inflexibility of institutionalization. This is what I feel we should be doing at the moment. I'm not saying that it would be valid politically to do this at all times.

So an anarchist society could not exist ?

No, I don't think so. We must look at Man as he is. Today's man is not capable of taking on the responsibilities of a society without any organization or authority. Man would not change at the wave of magic wand just because society becomes anarchistic. But I believe in the possibility of experimenting in small groups.

In what way is anarchism more compatible with Christianity than with Marxism ?

This question has given rise to a lot of discussion since it has been possible to derive a theological legitimacy to the power of the State from Christianity based on Paul's famous words, "All authority comes from God". Political power comes under constant criticism all the way through the Bible. For example, the people of Israel want a king, against the will of God. With surprising humour for the Bible, God remarks that a king would make soldiers of their sons, take their daughters for his harem and impose taxes. The Jews reply that nevertheless they want a king so as to have a leader like all the other peoples. There's criticism for you.

Next, Jesus's whole attitude seems to me to be a permanent condemnation of political power. The Apocalypse involves the destruction of political power. It's not for nothing that Rome fell ! I would interpret Paul as saying, "As Christians we are all against the State, but we should remember that authority also comes from

Chapter 1

God." In other words : "Don't be as violently against the State as you are being". Indeed the first generation of Christians were violently opposed to political authority.

It is sometimes said that your criticism of the 'technological society' is a sort of theoretical justification for a deep-rooted fear of the modern world. You are, as it were the archetypal reactionary, rejecting the State, technology, images, rejecting progress in short.

I am an historian, therefore I am perfectly well aware that we can never retrace our steps. I have no desire whatsoever to return to life in the Middle Ages. I have never been reactionary but I would like us to escape from this myth we have of progress. It is not at all obvious that people today are more intelligent, more enlightened or more moral than they were in Greece in the fifth century BC. The question that I ask myself is whether technological innovations will enable man to evolve in a positive sense or whether they may block the evolutionary process ?

If we take a historical perspective it is easy to see that man is becoming more and more independent and the individual has continually moved away from the group. This is particularly true in the Western world but is happening elsewhere as well. I see a sort of sharp decline in history and a negation of the individual, this is my observation as a sociologist. As a Christian my reaction is to call for a halt ! I am not suspicious of technology as such but I am very suspicious of the ways in which man uses it as an all-powerful instrument. We must go beyond the technological level at which we find ourselves today, we must find new forms of society and the technological means to re-establish a world fit to live in. But to achieve this we must first complete our critical analysis.

Where does your mistrust of images come from ? How can images pose a threat to the spoken work ?

In *La Parole Humiliée,* I tried to put together two ideas : the invasion of images and the devaluation of the spoken word. Today everything has a message and the spoken word is losing its force in a sea of words. In the Bible we are warned against trying to represent reality in case the representation is taken to be the real thing, no graven images. With regards to this book, it would be doubly wrong to think that I'm always criticizing modern society whereas it is in fact the image, which is stifling the word in modern society. Secondly, I do not belittle reality. I don't know how to think abstractly. I am not a philosopher and I have never understood the work of philosophers who only deal with ideas. I am a practical man and I was brought up in a visual world.

I do not belittle reality, but the Bible reminds us that the spoken word derives from the domain of truth whereas images derive from the domain of reality. The real must not be venerated as a truth, the idol - the image - must not be taken as God. God's image does not exist. God acts, creates solely through his words. God is a mystery, he cannot be known and he has chosen the medium of speech in order to be known. Jesus is the Word, God's spokesman, for the word exists in flesh and blood.

You were an environmentalist before your time. You must believe that the environment is losing its way today [2] in the 'political illusion'. Does this 'recuperation' have only perverse effects ? What assessment do you make of your own fight ?

To answer this I would refer to Bernard Charbonneau's [3] excellent critique of environmentalism. The environment is a fringe issue on the political agenda. I would consider it a disaster if the environmentalists came back into the political arena. What once happened with the Trades Unions will happen again, as soon as a group becomes politically active it divides up into a multitude of rival splinter groups. What is most important is that environmentalists should be asking the right questions.

Who is asking the right questions about the nuclear industry ?

In this domain, we are in the hands of the administrative authorities. People must understand the nature of this power before asking questions about how harmful it is. The technological bureaucrats who let us know, or conceal from us, the risks and the ideology involved in the nuclear industry are much more of a random factor than nuclear energy itself. Here, I agree with Marx who said that when man realizes that he no longer has the means of influencing the situation he begins to revolt.

And to find solutions ?

Not necessarily, but at least he is going the right way about finding them.

You systematically refute Marxism. Do you think that Marxism embraced Leninism ?

I don't think I criticize Marx in a negative way. I owe much of my intellectual development to him. He made me think. What I admire in Marx is his capacity to embrace new events. There is certainly a continuity from Marx to Lenin, but the Lenin in search of power was not the same Lenin when in power. The rupture took place there. He was a victim of his own power.

Was there ever an anti-authoritarian Marx ?

Yes, certainly.

But his methods : during the 1st Internationale for example ?

Chapter 1

You're right. But in fact, he was hoping to liberate man and in this respect he is anti-authoritarian. In other respects you should understand, when you are in a movement just how tempting it is to bring about the triumph of something you believe to be true and to sweep aside all obstacles.

In your opinion, the left has betrayed its own values : Western values. You also say that the right does not exist. In your eyes the right has neither legitimacy nor a future.

Look as long as you like you won't find the shadow of an idea, let alone any doctrine on the right. That might seem rather tough on the new philosophers, but ever since Maurras there has been nobody, no new ideas, only repetition.

There are certain scientific attitudes which could be viewed as rightwing.

No, it is the ideologists who transform scientific discoveries. It is not the scientists who champion the ideological repercussions of genetic engineering. But even if the traditional left has betrayed its initial vocation, it is nevertheless the left that offers us the best hopes for the future of humanity. Take, for example, my experience at the university. Every time I had an exceptionally gifted student, who wanted to know more, it was always a student from the classic left. That is the most striking facts to emerge over the last ten years. The left is our reservoir of intellectual potential for the future. The right has held, and continues to hold the reigns of power in a world that it cannot contain. The right always heads for disaster. That does not mean that a left-wing government would necessarily perform miracles.

Do you adhere to the Confucian idea that when man fails to find happiness he turns to pleasure ?

I notice that Western man is obsessed by happiness and that being well-off does not make him happy. Man believed that happiness was to be found in the complete absence of limits. We wanted non-directive education, but man is always very unhappy when he has no point of reference. He is like a rudderless boat. There is no Christian morality. There is a Revelation, at a given moment in time, from which Christians can derive a moral code in phase with the period in which they live, in which they live their faith.

Isn't your severity towards intellectuals and their moral obligations rather idealistic ?

Opinion-setters are accountable because of their influence and therefore if they cheat it is others who are cheated. I have no time for an intellectual who claims, "Yes, I was a Stalinist, I've said my mea culpa". How many youngsters has he already influenced ? If there is the slightest chance that we might be mistaken, we should not open our mouths.

Jacques Ellul

Does that mean you don't make mistakes ?

Oh ! Yes. Sometimes I have been wrong ! But not on matters where I might influence others. I have only tried to influence people when I was very sure of myself and in order to bring liberty to those to whom I was speaking.

You are often criticized for being pessimistic and Manichaean. You seem to enjoy swimming against the tide. Do you do this just for the sake of it ? Or rather, true to dialectical reasoning, you believe in the positivity of negativeness ?

First of all I am not at all Manichaean. As far as I am concerned, theologically speaking : all men are bad and all men are saved. I do not reason in terms of good and evil or of saved and damned, but in dialectic terms. Secondly, I gain no pleasure in going against the grain, but I firmly believe in the positivity of negativeness. Like Guéhenno I believe that man must first know how to say no, or like Descartes that man should accept nothing as fact before having examined it. My attitude is no more pessimistic than that of a doctor who, having seen the results of a patients tests, diagnoses cancer. I have always tried to warn people, to put them on their guard. I have always been convinced that man is free to initiate events other than those which seem to be inevitable.

In this society, does non-violence seem to you to be an effective counter force ? Is the State's monopoly of violence a good thing ?

Because of my spiritual convictions I am not only non-violent but I actually advocate meakness. Non-violence is certainly not an effective method. From a realistic point of view, force will always win. But for me, it is at this point that faith comes into the equation. Jesus Christ, who acted without force, ended up as one of the prime movers in history. God is on the side of the meek so they are the righteous but that does not mean that they succeed.

So you would say the means were an impediment to achieving the ends ?

It is not possible to build a just society with unjust means. It is impossible to create a free society based on slavery. These assertions lie at the heart of my reasoning.

---

[1] Forty-eight works in his life, without taking into account translations and re-editions.
[2] This interview was held in 1981.
[3] *Le Feu vert, Autocritique du mouvement écologiste*, Paris, Karthala, 1980.

CHAPTER TWO

An austere individual. Consecration post-mortem ? Work. Availability. The sin of pride. Specialization. Woe betide the polygraph. Presence in a modern world. Le Pen. Computer science. Socialism. Change revolutions. The Algerian war.

Patrick CHASTENET - *Would you consider yourself as someone austere ?*

JACQUES ELLUL - If I give that impression then I'm very sorry. I take great pleasure in food I enjoy good things. I'm absolutely not a puritan, I find Puritanism monstrous. I couldn't be described as an esthete because I'm a very committed person but I do love beautiful things and I'm particularly sensitive to art. On the one hand I find it very distressing to live in what I consider to be a tragic world but there again I have a cheerful disposition.

Do you sometimes regret that you never played the role of a leading thinker like Sartre, Ivan Illich or Marcuse ?

When I'm feeling low I do regret this. One is always sorry not to be able to influence the events of one's day. But I have no regrets when I assess the value of their influence in terms of the way things really are. I know what kinds of misunderstandings such fads are based on.

Several theses have already been written on your work and your ideas are taught in certain American universities. Do you derive any satisfaction from the fact that you are a French thinker who is held in higher esteem in Berkeley than in Paris ? Do you believe that one day the French intelligentsia will stop giving you the cold shoulder ?

Yes. When I'm dead. If French civilization still exists ten or fifteen years from now [1], they will appreciate what I've written. There has always been a long delay before my books have caught on. I blame this on the centralization of everything on Paris, which is something I have often criticized. My work is well-considered abroad. So I feel sure that one day I will be understood here in France.

When you work ten hours a day as you do, is there any time left over to give to those things you value so highly namely friendship and love ? Or do you merely live with the intention of spending time on them ?

That is a very cruel question. I acknowledge that I have imposed an ascetic life on my wife and that my children have suffered from this too. Qualitatively the time that I have for those near and dear to me is essential. I sometimes feel I am like a tight-rope walker. I live by a very strict timetable which does mean that I can work well but also that in an emergency I can be completely available.

You have stated that a Christian should live his life according to what he believes.

That is correct. I believe I can honestly say that I have never turned away anyone who asked me a serious question. But this has led to situations that were rather surreal. I would be receiving someone while all the time there was the nagging thought at the back of my mind of a book I was trying to finish. Fortunately I've always been a fast worker. Thanks to my good health I was always able to put in ten hours work a day. Unfortunately over the last three years [2] I've only been able to do half that, which is very tiresome. I believe that God commanded me to do this work and I have put my intelligence at his service !

Like certain Marxist writers when asked to justify why they have withdrawn from the world, won't you have to answer that your "praxis" lies in your theoretical activities ?

I would reply with my motto of twenty years ago "Think globally act locally." I have always been actively involved in local issues e.g. meetings of the Esprit Club, the French Resistance, crime prevention hostels, campaigning to save the Atlantic Coast. I am not a philosopher who deals in general ideas but with real issues concerning others.

You give the impression that your life is all planned out. Where do improvisation and spontaneity enter into it ?

I am never spontaneous. Everything is thought out and under control. Even as a child I was self-contained. I never let myself go. I've written several books of poetry none of which have been published [3]. My children can do that if they wish after my death. I, personally, cannot put myself on display.

Don't you commit the sin of pride by going after recognition and glory ?

Certainly not after glory. If I'd been after that I'd have gone about it differently. At the age of twenty-two Bernard Charbonneau and I wondered about going into politics as a career, we both would have been pretty competent at it. We decided against it however. As far as writing is concerned I know exactly what kind of stupid ideas to put together to be able to sell between fifty and one hundred thousand copies. Nevertheless it is true that I am very proud ! As a Christian I know that one should try and fight pride and for years I tried to do so. The more one strives to be humble the more one's pride is fueled. Today I have overcome my pride,

Chapter 2

but so saying it is very arrogant to make such a claim. I admit that I am guilty of pride. Now it is a matter for the Almighty to judge and it is no longer my concern.

Why didn't you content yourself with being at the University ? Why did you seek out a broader public through journalism ?

Charbonneau and I had given up the idea of going into politics but we had not given up the idea of changing the world. We were of the opinion that the average reader was much more discerning than the world of journalism generally realized. It was simply a matter of presenting the reader with complex issues written in a straightforward fashion. Quite a challenge for an academic to make himself understood by the uninitiated !

At a time when it was fashionable to be a specialist in something the fact that you had a variety of poles of interest must have been held against you.

There is nothing worse than someone who publishes in different fields. My books on theology were implicitly acknowledged as being serious by the best theologians but were never quoted in their bibliographies. Similarly my books in political science were treated with suspicion. As a Christian I feel I have work to do and things to say in both fields.

In a society like ours the authorities, be they right or left-wing, perceive people like me as dangerous individuals because we are in a position to criticize from the perspective of several disciplines. The present trend in universities is towards more and more specializaton. Personally I have suffered from this attitude as the story I am about to tell will show.

My university career was pretty abysmal. I was never selected on merit for promotion. The only promotion I had was on seniority. One day I went to complain about a colleague being promoted ahead of me once again, this particular one had not published a word in twenty years. Professor LeBras, a clever, witty fellow, answered me as follows "My dear friend you should realize you are being penalized, not for not doing what you are paid to do, but for what you are doing in fields in which you are not paid." It's quite true I did not stick slavishly to my speciality.

You criticize the Church for not fulfilling its true role in the modern world. You do not advocate it should withdraw into contemplation however...

The Church should be revolutionizing the world towards freedom. The mistake has been of equating revolution with Stalinism or Maoism and thinking that revolution can only be brought about at the end of a gun. Power can be won in this way, but never freedom. We are going to have to find a completely new way to go about achieving freedom, one far removed from the traditional context.

Isn't that being a little Utopian ?

The proof that it's not is provided by the way young people are reacting to traditional politics, they simply couldn't care less.

Do you think this is something to rejoice about ? Whenever people are indifferent or turn from politics most unfortunate events often follow. Could we say that the general lassitude towards politics today may be to the advantage of the likes of Jean-Marie Le Pen ? Is that progress ?

Distrust of politics doesn't mean indifference to society. I myself have often fought against professional politicians. As for Le Pen, and I am not one to hand out lables lightly, I would say that he is the typical *fascist*. There is the cult of strength, morality, and he's always harping on about Christian values and xenophobia.

Recently [4] you caused quite a stir when you stated that the socialist revolution was possible. Socialist revolution is a rather hackneyed phase what do you mean by it ?

I'm not keen on inventing words, this statement has already earned me quite a few attacks. The word "socialism" remains exact. What has to be done is put the power back into the hands of society and away from the people who have been monopolizing it i.e. the politicians. I am for socialism with personal freedom which is only possible in small groups. Information technology could be used to form the link between different groups so that they could be co-ordinated at a global level. This could only be achieved in stages. Sadly I believe that there is but the slimmest of chances that this form of socialism will ever see the light of day.

Hence *Changer de révolution* ("Change revolutions") is the bleakest of all my books. So saying the present state of confusion cannot continue for ever. We will either have to bring about a radical mutation of our society or we'll be swallowed up into a dictatorship. There are times in History when it is possible to change things and the present situation is fluid and therefore suitable.

Is it in the name of some mythical ideal that you refuse to come down in favor of either of the two major protagonists of today ? The lesser of two evils is...

If I had to choose between living under the domination of the Americans or the Soviets, I'd prefer the Americans. But I would stay free. If I were to adopt the Western line I would feel free to criticize it. I would not tolerate the setting up of a Soviet-style political police in America. Some people think that it is dreadful that I level my criticism at my friends, my church or at my own side. To get back to capitalism and liberalism both concepts are based on the principles of competition and this is contrary to what I believe in. As you know Christ teaches us that we should respect our weaker brethren not try to beat them.

So Christians will systematically place themselves on the opposite side ?

Man's first duty is to be critical without hurting his fellow man.

Chapter 2

With a certain hindsight, does this throw light on the stand you took during the Algerian war ?

My position in 1954 was that we should liberalize immediately, that we should give Algeria an independent status and dual nationality to all Algerians. We couldn't go on saying that Algeria was France but on the other hand we couldn't simply write off one and a half million Algerian-born Frenchmen, whose families had lived there for several generations in many cases and who considered Algeria as their country. So after 1956 when everyone started tearing each other apart I refused to take sides.

Were you close to Camus ?

Yes, very close indeed. My position was badly construed because nearly all Protestant intellectuals were in favor of the Algerian Freedom Fighters. According to me the Christian way is to step in while the situation is still fluid to try to play a mediating role.

---

[1] This interview took place in 1984.
[2] Idem.
[3] **Silences,** Editions OPALES, Bordeaux, 1995.
[4] In *Changer de révolution* published by Seuil in 1982.

CHAPTER THREE

Father. Mother. Genealogy. Origins. An aristocrat. Sense of honour. The Obrenovic's. Malta. The Jewish calender. The Austro-Hungarian Empire. Pierre Mendès France. Political realism. Christians and politics. No war is just. The power of the "bureaux". The Bible.

Patrick CHASTENET - *You were born in Bordeaux in 1912, could you tell me some more about your origins ?*

JACQUES ELLUL - I was indeed born on the 6th of January 1912 but it was somewhat by chance that I was born in Bordeaux. My father came from the port town of Trieste which at that time belonged to Austria. He did all his studies in Vienna. After doing brilliantly at the law school and then at the business school he was given a grant to go to Bordeaux for one year to get work experience with a trading company. They found him so efficient, he spoke five languages into the bargain, that at the end of the training period they wanted to keep him. That is how my father became an authorized representative for Louis Eschenauer, a big wine merchant. That is also how he came to settle in Bordeaux and meet my mother.

My mother's mother was French thus bringing my family its only French element. My mother's father was Portuguese probably of Portuguese Jewish descent, his name was Mendès. So I owe my existence to an encounter between a Portuguese woman and an Austrian which took place in Bordeaux.

Another interesting feature of their relationship was that when my father fell in love with my mother he had a good job, was able to spend money and was leading a carefree bachelor life. She was a young woman of slender means, made even more slender because she had to support a widowed mother with no income whatsoever and two sisters, one with tuberculosis and the other was blind. All that these four women had to live on came from what my mother was able to earn by giving drawing and painting lessons.

I have no idea how my parents met. The fact remains that my father fell in love with my mother even though during those first years he must have come across young women who were more beautiful and certainly much richer than her. They married in 1907.

What do you know about your father's roots ?

He himself was an Austrian subject although his mother was Serbian and his father Italian. My father valued honour over and about everything else. He got this from his own father. I'll tell you one of our family tales that we used to tell over and over again. My father's father was a rich Trieste ship-owner with four vessels to his name. One of these vessels sank, one was captured and a third had its cargo damaged. This all happened around 1892-1894. He wasn't sufficiently insured so he was forced to go bankrupt. He preferred death to dishonour and so committed suicide.

On learning this my grandmother, who incidentally was a descendant of Obrenovic' - one of the first Kings of Serbia at the beginning of the nineteenth century - went into mourning and when still a young woman withdrew into a little house which she never left until she died.

My father conserved a very aristocratic attitude and I grew up in that atmosphere. He was an aristocrat through and through, but he was an aristocrat without privileges or means, indeed he had become nothing more than a trader and little by little his life became very difficult because he had an impossible personality.

Was you father considered as an Austrian during the war ?

No, things were much more complicated than that. My father was English because his father had been born in Malta. Under English law a British citizen can never lose his nationality. So my father had been registered as British when he arrived in Bordeaux in 1902.

The name Ellul is Maltese but it does have a Hebrew ring to it, doesn't it ?

Yes indeed. "Elul" spelt with one l is the name of a month on the Hebrew calender. But it seems it is also an Arab name as well as being Jewish and there is also a Catholic version of it which can be seen on the tomb of an archdeacon called Ellul in the cathedral in Malta. The Ellul family which was quite a tribe in Malta was broken up when the English occupied the island in 1802. My grandfather left for Trieste and the others were scattered all around the world. To my knowledge I have distant cousins in Tunisia and in Brazil.

Has the fact that your name could be thought Jewish had any affect on you ?

Not at all. I have never thought of myself as Jewish and during the war I was never investigated because of my name.

What influence did your parents have on your intellectual career and spiritual development ?

My father was a sceptic and an admirer of Voltaire consequently he was a tolerant man. For example he wouldn't let me have any religious instruction but he would let me read the Bible at home.

I have already mentioned he valued honour above everything. As he told me so many times, to be a man of honour does not involve simply making a point of honour it means never letting your friends down, always being available to the poor and always standing up to powerful forces.

Chapter 3

His particular code of honour was to cost him a great deal and prevented him from ever having a steady job. While he was employed by Eschenauer, for example, he found it very hard to stand the extreme language of his boss. One day, in the presence of outsiders, Louis Eschenauer was rude to him. My father demanded a public apology which he got. But also got fired.

There were several occasions when my father would put his honour before his own interest. During the First World War, while he was working as chief accountant for quite a big Bordeaux firm, he came across a number of irregularities, in particular he discovered that the firm was sending out cans of rotten food to the soldiers. He lost no time in denouncing this publicly. Naturally he was fired on the spot. Little by little he slipped down the social ladder as a result of his absolutely uncompromising personality.

My father lost his job for the third time in 1929. He was to stay unemployed for more than a year. At this point we found ourselves in dire straits. All we had to live on came from my mother's painting and the odd private lessons I was able to give in French, Latin or Greek.

Was your mother a professional painter ?

She was a art teacher. After the Great War lots of families wanted portraits of their sons or relatives who had fallen in battle. So my mother was able to make her living painting these portraits for quite some time. She also taught painting in a private school and gave painting lessons at home.

What did your mother's parents do ?

Her father was in the wine trade selling Porto, her mother didn't work. I never knew either of them.

Did you know your father's family at all ?

No. All I do know is that my father had fallen out with his brother and that he had no time for his sister, whose sole aim in life was to marry well. She actually achieved her goal, she eventually married into a grand family belonging to the Austro-Hungarian aristocracy. I should point out that my father depised the Austro-Hungarian Empire. He always felt more Italian than anything else. When he was a student he belonged to the Italia Irredenta movement that was fighting for the liberation of Trentin and Trieste.

Did he have very strong political views ?

Not at all. He did judge people however. He had a lot of respect for Clémenceau and he had none for Briand. He was more interested in the personality and the political achievement of a politician than his doctrinal beliefs.

So he admired men who could be decisive, men with strong personalites ?

That's right. He liked leaders.

You yourself are drawn to that kind of personality, aren't you. Despite your anarchist leanings.

What I did admire in de Gaulle was his rallying call of the 18th of June and the way he behaved in the Resistance. But I strongly disapproved of his politics after the Liberation. In other words I have never been able to admire any charismatic leader whatsoever. On the contrary I have always felt suspicious whenever a politician begins presenting himself as a great leader.

On the other hand the person I most liked during that whole period was Mendès France. He never had any pretentions of being the saviour of the nation or of playing a providential role. My break with de Gaulle stems from the fact that immediately after the war he placed his confidence in Pleven and not in Mendès France. That was a crazy thing to do.

Mendès France's popularity was inversely proportional to the time he spent in office, wouldn't you say ?

Mendès wasn't in power long that's true but he always had an extremely honest line of conduct. He always did what he said he would do and he always informed us about what he intended to do, without fear of ridicule. In as far as it is possible for a politician to do so he did manage to avoid falling into the trap of making deals or getting involved in dubious business. And that is what I admired about him. Moreover he didn't hang onto power long and that is also a sign of this worth.

Did you know him personally ?

I did meet him once in Bordeaux, it was a very friendly occasion as it happens. It was shortly after he had left office and I remember him saying, in substance, that : "I've had enough. I spend my days avoiding ambushes and traps that have been laid for me and I simply no longer have time to think about serious politics."

On the one hand you have shown that politics is the domain of division and illusion, and on the other hand you have always advocated realism in concrete situations. But, surely since the time of Machiavelli, we have been aware of the discrepancy that exists between Christian or Humanist qualities and political qualities ?

I've often reproached my Christian friends with that. How many times have we found ourselves in political situations where dreadful decisions have to be taken if we want to be serious. Intellectually, I would have been able to conceive of these

Chapter 3

decisions but, psychologically, I would have been unable to carry them out. So it was just as well that I never went into politics.

According to me, once you have decided to go to war you have to go all out and use every means at your disposal. This is the case that applied in Algeria. Everyone was shouting their heads off against the torture that was going on. But the real problem was not the torture but the war itself. There is no morality in war. If you want to win you must pull out all the stops.

My view is that war falls into the domain of necessity. Consequently it is diammetrically opposite to what I would wish for mankind, namely freedom. There is no freedom in war. There is no freedom to choose to act or to choose not to act. You are only allowed to do those things which will win the war.

I can hear the anti-military activist in you speaking there. You claim that when one goes to war no holds must be barred but also that there is never any justification for going to war. Isn't your point of view a little excessive?

What is true is that there has never been a just war. Be under no illusion about that. All wars are unjust if only because of the means one has to use to wage them. The very objectives that one is trying to achieve are rendered unjust by virtue of the means one uses. All wars engender other wars.

Was it political realism that led you to be pro-Munich?

I defended the Munich agreements because, as I have written elsewhere, it was either "too late or too soon" to enter the war. It was too late in that the moment when we should have blocked Hitler was in 1935 when he reoccupied the Rhine, at that stage we would have won easily. It was too soon in that, as I saw things, if we had waited a little longer we would have had the time to get properly armed.

But this is purely a realistic political standpoint, I personally would never have been able to implement that kind of politics.

How would you define your relation to politics?

I first became involved in politics at the Liberation when I heard the slogan "Forward from the Resistance to the Revolution". We were convinced that we would be able to bring about a deep change in society through politics because society was in a very malleable state straight after the war. Our hopes were to be thwarted.

From my practical experience as a delegate councillor on the interim city council in Bordeaux, I found that I had virtually no real control over what went on in the administrative offices. In concrete terms, and this happened time and time again, as I had several departments under my orders I had to rubber stamp dossiers that were presented to me without sufficient information being available about them. I would sign thirty letters a day for which I only really had any knowledge of about ten dossiers at most.

So I asked myself: "Under conditions like these how on earth do ministers manage? For the three hundred or so letters that they sign each day just how many of the related dossiers must they never even set eyes on ?" I absolutely have to have all the information on a topic before I can work on it, so it was clear to me that I was not cut out for a life in politics.

Isn't that a rather sweeping generalization based on a rather limited personal experience ?

That's always been my way of working. I've always based my reflections on personal experiences. From there I've tested out my ideas by trying to find arguments to contradict or fault them.

So you proceed in three stages. You start from an isolated experience namely your own. In the next stage you seek out any couter-arguments and then you compare your analyses with those of your intellectual or academic colleagues ?

Precisely.

I feel we have gone rather astray from the subject we were discussing which was your parents' influence on you. Can we get back to that, do you think ?

Of course. First of all, like it or not, I inherited a strong aristocratic and deep-rooted sense of honour from my father. My respect for my father knew no bounds. But I would never say that our relationship was an affectionate one.

Was he gentle with you, did he kiss you ?

Yes, of course he did. But with what reserve ! It was really.... Should we say, whenever we heard my father's footsteps when he came home, everything had to be in its place, my toys had to be out of the way and I would be almost standing to attention.

Was he a big man, physically ?

No he was small. He was about as tall as I am now. He was not imposing by virtue of his physical stature but by virtue of his penetrating stare, which everyone found very intimidating. At mealtimes for example no-one would ever have dreamed of contradicting him during a discussion.

How old was he when you were born ?

He must have been forty and my mother was thirty-three. My mother was very artistic, extremely modest, very hard-working and held her husband in enormous esteem. She never taught me how to pray, she never tried to influence me in religious matters because she had promised her husband that she wouldn't. Simply I would see her kneeling down to pray each evening. I used to ask her what she was doing and she would reply that she was praying. Nothing more.

Chapter 3

She had made my father a promise and she was sufficiently honest to keep it. One day, I must have been eighteen or nineteen, I had been reading the Bible quite a lot, had become passionate about it and believed in Jesus Christ, I went to find her in the kitchen and said to her : "Do you know something, Mother ? I believe in Jesus Christ and I have converted." She replied without even turning round that she was not at all surprised and that she had been praying each night for that to happen even since I was born.

This is most extraordinary when you consider that she was a woman driven by such faith and yet she had managed to keep her word, without flinching for so long. She never attended services, she never went to see the minister she conducted her faith alone.

Were her parents Christians ?

Her father was Catholic and her mother Protestant.

Was the fact that you chose to belong to the reformed faith due to your reading of the Bible or the indirect influence of your mother ?

It's complicated. Basically I would say that its due to my reading of the Bible. In the Bible I discovered a sort of truth or obviousness that I found nowhere else. In my second year at University I was contacted by a fellow student who knew of my mother's faith. He invited me to join the Protestant student association. It was as a member of this association I came under the influence of Protestantism.

After that I proceeded in my usual way by putting my ideas to test through reading Catholic writers. I thought to myself : "It's not just because my Protestant friends are nice that they are right." So I set about reading the works of Catholic theologians. Then I came to the conclusion that the interpretations of Protestant writers seemed closer to the way I understood the Bible.

CHAPTER FOUR

Childhood memories. The Jardin Public. A good fight. Secular State schoolboys versus those from private Catholic schools. Friendship. Roaming around. The Bordeaux quays. The navy or the law ? The Arcachon bassin. The canoe. Top of the class. Bordeaux smart society. Cold and calculating. Lead soldiers. The army. An obvious candidate for reform. Unpublished poetry. Introspection. A man like any other. Psychoanalysis.

Patrick CHASTENET - *What is your earliest recollection ?*

Jacques ELLUL - It must have been in 1914 when I was two and a half. I was playing in the park, the Jardin Public, and I remember being drawn towards the sound of music, military music, when I saw some soldiers coming towards us carrying rifles and my mother saying to me : "Look at them they are soldiers going off to the war". Then I don't really know what got hold of me but I went over to a flower-bed picked a small bunch of flowers and took it over to one of the soldiers and said : "Here soldier this is for you".

I remember that he then took me in his arms and kissed me. I was extremely moved by that procession. Naturally at that age I had no idea what war was but I did understand that something extremely serious was going on.

Which were you favourite places in Bordeaux ?

The Jardin Public was where I loved to spend my time. We lived very close by, in a road that is now called the rue Emile Zola but at that time went under the name of rue Bardineau after the famous Bordeaux chef.

When I was really small I went to the Jardin Public with my mother and it was to become the scene of many important events that affected me as I was growing up. I played there with my friends. I fought there with them too. Goodness how we loved a good fight it was fantastic !

I thought of you as an only child brought up by an overprotective mother rather than a gang leader.

When I was at the lycée I was small and not very strongly-built. At the age of eight or nine I was bullied by boys who took advantage of the fact that they were very much stronger than me. I puzzled over my predicament and the thought came to me : "Alone I've had it, but what if three or so of us form a group together ? When one of us was picked on the other two could rush to his side We would surely be able to defend ourselves like that !"

I thereupon recruited the two other small boys in the class and we made a pact together. From that moment on we stopped being attacked by the big boys. This anecdote is pretty typical of how I was in the lycée and in the Jardin Public.

Indeed not much later on when I was about 12 or 13 and by this time at the lycée Longchamp [1] we would wage "state versus church" battles of heroic proportions. There were two rival gangs one from the state, therefore secular, school and the other from the collège Tivoli, a Catholic school. At appointed hours we met on the terrace of the Jardin Public to engage in pitched battles whirling clubs, hurling stones and whatever else we could sling... it was pretty spectacular.

Tell us more about the personality of the young Ellul ?

As an adolescent what I was really looking for was one or two true friends, and I found them. I was extraordinarily lucky to have a friend whom I loved with all my heart, I can quite honestly say that there was never any homosexual dimension to the relationship. This was an extremely pure friendship with a boy from a working class background called Pierre Farbos. We were as close as two brothers.

Which year was this ?

We first met at the beginning of secondary school. I found a brother in him. There was one moment when we nearly broke up that was when he decided to go to Saint-Cyr, the military academy. I was very antimilitary. However if you were a clever pupil from a poor background, Saint-Cyr was the fastest way to get a decent place in the working world. He went ahead and passed the entrance exam and despite this difference of opinion we remained firm friends.

We met everyday. We spent all our time together even during the holidays. Our principal pastime was roaming around. Whenever we had a free moment we roamed the quays which at that time where not guarded. We helped ourselves to peanuts, cocoabeans indeed anything the porters happened to spill from the sacks they had slung across their backs. From time to time we dipped in directly to grab the loot.

Pierre Farbos and I also got into some rather interesting situations. Whenever we had a few coins scraped together we would treat ourselves to a couple of shandies at the "Three Sisters Bar", near the warehouses, down-river. As perhaps its name would suggest this was not a place of high repute. Indeed I saw the "sisters". They were rather nice I must say. We understood perfectly what happened when they went upstairs. But they never once bothered us, even though we were young teenage boys. They were really decent with us. I have never felt any revulsion for this kind of woman and this early experience probably explains why. I learned never to make moral judgements.

Apart from the Jardin Public and the quays ?

We used to go on long outings Eysines. Today the whole area it built up but in those days it was given over to market gardening. There was a large area to the

Chapter 4

north-east of Bordeaux known as the Cressonnière. It was a marshland which was partially-drained into hundreds of small streams. These marshes and the extraordinary wild-life from the streams provided Pierre and I with untold discoveries and adventures.

What is really most extraordinary is that my mother never seemed to worry about the dangers we could run into along the quays or far into the marshland areas of the Cressonnière. I used to go off at two in the afternoon and never get back till around seven. I was allowed total freedom to do as I pleased, as long as I had learned my lessons and finished my homework. I had an incredibly unfettered childhood. I experienced a degree of freedom that few children today could even image.

Was Farbos a member of your mutual defence pact ?.

Indeed yes. He was one of the small boys. He was my height and about my size. The third member was a chap called Hérault. He was very nice but wasn't in the same class as Farbos who after all did become an air marshal later on in life.

Do you think that your roaming could have developed into delinquency ?

No. We never stole, apart from the odd peanut of course. We were simply on the look out for the unexpected. The quays at that time were wonderful to watch. I remember the breathtaking sight of the sails of the cod fleet as it came and went. We wouldn't have missed that for anything.

You were very drawn to the sea and to boats, weren't you ?

(Laughs) Very much so. I actually chose some of my studies so that I could become a navy officer. When I was fifteen my father said to me "You are going to read law my boy". When my father said something there was no arguing. I was pretty furious but there was nothing I could do.

Was he somewhat of a tyrant at home ?

Absolutely not, because he never said anything. He never made a show of authority because his authority was automatic. I would say that my mother and I held him in the same respect as that reserved for the king at the time of the monarchy. It went without saying.

He never lost his temper.

(Laughs) Yes sometimes but over very unimportant matters. Even when we were rather poor he always dressed to the nines. If ever his detachable collars were not starched just so he would go off the deep end.

So he upset your plans to join the navy ?

Yes he did by forcing me to read law. The next day I went to him and said "If I read law I warn you I intend to go to the bitter end" To which he replied "Do what you like as long as you read law". He had himself studied law for a while and was fascinated by legal problems.

Even though your father made you give up plans to join the navy he didn't manage to kill your passion for the sea, did he ?

I've always been in love with the sea and I've been able to share this passion with my wife who is even more enthusiastic about it than I am.

Did you ever sail a yacht ?

No at that time no-one did. Altogether, in the whole of the Arcachon bassin, there was only one eight-meter boat owned by the Rothschilds, perhaps a dozen six-meter-fifties and ten or so six-meters. Thanks to the family of one of my friends who had taken pity on me, should we say, from the age of fourteen or so I was invited to Canon on the Arcachon basin and there I was able sail for a month each year. The boat I used was called a "pinasse" which is basically a rowing boat but you can also fit it with a sail.

I believe you also went canoeing ?

Indeed I did. But that was much later on, after the war when I was able to buy my very own canoe. I became quite famous locally because of the amount of canoeing I went in for and the dangerous exploits I undertook. My wife and I used to canoe out into the open sea, navigating across dangerous channels, we went everywhere.

To get back to your studies. You passed your school leaving exam at sixteen, I believe. Were you what we call today a gifted child ?

I was a very good pupil. I got the form prize every year until I was entered my last lycée, but these good results were entirely due to the exceptional dedication of my mother. For example on entering secondary school, I began Latin, so Mother set herself to learning it at the same time.

Which were your favourite subjects ?

French, Latin, Greek, history and recitation. I was hopeless at math.

You seem to fit the stereotype one finds in books or sees at the cinema of the top of the form, don't you ?

Chapter 4

I was very unruly for a top-of-the-form-type. Most of the time the teachers were very decent with me I had such good marks that they didn't punish me. I didn't work in order to be top of the form. I worked because I loved what I was doing. The lycée Longchamp didn't teach the higher classes so I moved to the lycée Montaigne and there I was outclassed.

I found myself in a truly exceptional form and my class-mates were much better than me. Suddenly I found myself in fourth or fifth position which came as a shock as I had never experienced such a thing before. I tried my hardest but I never got back to the top again. I was very disappointed I can tell you.

Did your academic success help your family move closer to polite society ?

Quite the contrary. When I got my school leaving diploma a very well-intentioned lady from the Bordeaux high society called on my mother and said to her : "Madame Ellul, we know that your son did extremely well at his final exam and also we know that you are in financial difficulties. We would like to offer Jacques a well-paid job in our firm." To which my mother replied : "My son is far too gifted to go into trade. He'll do something completely different and certainly will not be following in his father's footsteps."

Did you have the impression that you were snubbed by the Protestant bourgeoisie ?

Not at all. I was totally indifferent to that world. Obviously when I was at law school I did run into some well-connected students in the University Protestant association.

Now that you have become famous, do you feel that you belong to this group of people who live off their inheritance, after all your religion is something you have in common with these well-heeled Protestants ?

No I don't belong, even though some of my best friends do belong to these powerful families like Edouard and René Kressmann or Edmond Cruse. However when I was young I never had anything to do with people from that world, I simply never ran into them. When I was twenty for instance I was once invited to a society ball. I found the whole thing deadly boring because I didn't know how to dance. This left me with no wish whatsoever to repeat the experience.

You once described yourself as being "cold and calculating". Is this true ?

I would say so. Even though I am very moved by poetry for example. I am both very passionate and very cold. I would describe myself as being cold insofar as I cannot help distancing myself from events. When I take part in social gatherings I do so wholeheartedly, I share the emotions of those who are close to me and afterwards I "ponder the matter". I try to analyse why certain things had been said and done.

Jacques Ellul

What would you say has changed in your character over the years?

I have become more open towards other people this has happened under the influence of Christianity and of my wife. At sixteen I was a little brute interested in absolutely no-one except my friend Farbos and I was an absolute glutton for work. Work and books were my passion. You mustn't forget I was an only child.

In your spare time did you have a typical loner's activities?

Not as far as my taste for a good fight was concerned. But it is true that I did have a hobby which was rather unusual for a antimilitary type like me (laughs). I would spend whole afternoons making lead soldiers. I would take the little lead figures and work on them with a soldering iron. Then I would paint them taking care to be absolutely faithful to real-life uniforms because I was already deeply fascinated by history. I can show you my collection, I still have it. I believe it must be rather unique.

Tell me about your relationship with the Army.

My relationship with the Army was quite unusual. In my time every student had to attend the reserve officer training college. Now I was quite adamant if I did anything at all I would only accept to be an ordinary soldier but wouldn't dream of being an officer. There was a catch in this. It wasn't possible to take any exams if one wasn't signed up for that special military training. So somehow I managed to get myself thrown out of the programme and being thus disqualified I became qualified to sit the exams.

The outcome of all this was that I was sent, not to a disciplinary regiment, but to Orleans with a bunch of tough guys. My life as an ordinary soldier in the company of these young men, who were virtually all delinquants, was absolutely abominable. I suffered all kinds of harrasment, ragging and abuse in that dreadful unit. It was so bad in fact that when I ran into a captain by chance in the barracks parade ground, some four months into my service, he asked me if I was ill.

Indeed I was unsteady on my feet and I looked so awful that, not satisfied with my reply, he ordered me off to the sick-bay to be looked at. From there I was transfered to hospital where I was found to be so exhausted the doctors decided that I should be reformed for a while. Subsequently this temporary reform became definitive.

Had you finished your studies?

All this happened during the academic year 1934-35. I had passed my degree taken my qualfying exam and was embarked on my doctorate.

Do you see yourself as an austere and undemonstraive Calvinist?

Chapter 4

First of all I am not a Calvinist. I am a follower of Karl Barth who was just the opposite. He was joyful and warm-hearted. Calvin wanted to introduce an unshakeable logic into a domain that I consider not as intellectual. I can't go along with that.

But you were a Calvinist at the outset ?

No. I was much more influenced by Luther and by Kierkegaard than I ever was by Calvin. I've studied Calvin (Laughs). When I was reading theology I was landed with the task of writing a critical summary of Book IV of the *Christian Institutes*. I read the whole work and believe me I found it deadly boring. I have never been attracted by that kind of rigour.

You would agree, wouldn't you, that you are rather cold, even though this does not stem from your spiritual convictions ?

Yes. Despite the fact that I am Latin I am not demonstrative.

How do you account for this reserve ?

I would say that it comes from the distance that existed in my feelings for my father. He was always extremely kind with me but he was never demonstrative. I suppose I've followed his example.

I can't put my finger on it but I feel that you are leaving something out when you describe the influence of your parents.

Perhaps I should have mentioned that my mother passed on her love of poetry to me. Fortunately I always had intelligent teachers who let us choose our own recitation texts. Mother, who adored poetry, always guided me towards the better poets. From the age of six or seven I have had a taste for poetry. Poetry is the art form which pleases me the most and in which I find deep meaning.

Have you ever thought of publishing your own poems ?

No [2]. I believe I've told you before if my heirs feel like publishing my notebooks of poems, if they feel it's a good idea, they can. That is the way I am. In poetry one bares one's soul and I don't like baring my soul.

For those of us who have read your "What I believe" *it is clear that you do not like confessions.*

Quite honestly I have to tell you that I am not enormously interested in myself. For example I've never been able to stand Proust's style. All that business of writhing tormented souls, tearing things to shreds, and going deeper ever deeper, it all leaves me stone cold. I may not be demonstrative but I am very outward-looking.

But surely in order to understand others you must also understand yourself? Is introspective work necessarily self-satisfying?

That is what I have always experienced, even in sociology. I watch a film or a T.V. program and feel this or that about what I've seen. My feelings are spontaneous, I'm a very good audience. It is afterwards that I start to turn it over in my mind.

I analyse my own feelings which I later transpose. I use myself as a model of the average man, usually I react like any man in the street. I'm rarely mistaken, quite simply because I'm well-equipped intellectually and that I don't consider myself as being different in any way.

Your intellectual achievements do rather set you aside from the common herd.

I really do believe that I am like everybody else. What rather backs this up is the fact that so many people say to me having read one of my books "It really is extraordinary, you have written exactly what I think."

Are you sure that's not just false modesty?

Oh no. Modesty is not my strong point ! (Laughs)

Would you say that introspection is dangerous or useless?

That doesn't interest me at all. I have only been successful in fields that interest me. I'm not in the least bit interested to know who I am.

In that case, what about psychoanalysis?

I'm extremely suspicious of psychoanalysis since so many of its victims have passed through my hands, if you'll pardon the expression. In my ministry I've come across so many poor souls who have been spiritually and psychologically destroyed by psychoanalysis that I have retained a certain distrust for the practice. Nevertheless, Jung and Adler have helped me in my sociology work unlike Freud.

---

[1] Later to become the lycée Montesquieu.
[2] Several months before his death Jacques Ellul accepted to entrust his poetry notebooks to the publishing house OPALES.

CHAPTER FIVE

The absolute. The Bible. Conversion. A matter between God and myself. School-minded. Goethe. Tacitus. Kierkegaard. Dialectics. Marx. Politics in the lycée. Girls and boys. Law school. Camping in the Pyrénées. Maurice Duverger. The Jèze strikes. A Dutch-looking girl.

Patrick CHASTENET - *What was your most characteristic trait when you were an adolescent ?*

Jacques ELLUL - I would say that my marked taste for the absolute would characterize me pretty well at that age. I saw everything in absolutely clearcut terms. I was looking for a truth that would be wholly satisfactory for me. In a way one could say that it was inevitable that I would run into Christianity.

At what age did you discover the Bible ?

I began reading the Bible at the age of seven or eight. It was a book that I found fascinating. Of course there were lots of things I didn't understand in it.

Don't you think that that is rather normal for an eight-year-old ?

It wasn't the actual content that I had trouble understanding. In the version of the Bible that we had at home some words were printed in italics. I asked my mother what that meant. She was unable to come up with an answer so she sent me off to a preacher she knew. I took my Bible along to show him but he couldn't give me an answer either. I was very disappointed and put a second question to him.
There's a passage in the Bible where God says he will spare all those he loves for a thousand generations but those who sin against him he will punish for three generations. I asked the preacher to explain to me how the calculation worked. What happens if in the middle of the thousand generations one man should disobey, this would imply that the next three generations should be punished, in which case what happens to the remaining five hundred generations who were entitled to be spared ? He just stood there dumb struck, unable to answer this my second question. At which point I felt extremely frustrated and I said to myself : "You're going to have to manage on your own. Grown-ups simply don't understand anything." This episode pretty well illustrates how I would read the Bible later on.

So you felt frustrated but you didn't feel let down ? You didn't lose faith in the Bible but in adults. You could so easily have decided that the Bible was nonsense or illogical and turned your back on it, couldn't you ?

As a historian there were too many things in it that I found fascinating. For a start with there was the tremendous history of the Jews and there were passages in the Gospels that moved me deeply. Whenever I had got my work out of the way before dinner I would sit down and read a passage of the Bible for the sheer pleasure of it.

When and how did your conversion occur ?

I would have preferred not to talk about that. When it did occur it was overwhelming I would even say violent. It happened during the summer holidays. I was staying with friends in Blanquefort not far from Bordeaux. I must have been seventeen at the time as I had just taken my final exams at school. I was alone in the house busy translating Faust when suddenly, and I have not doubts on this at all, I knew myself to be in the presence of a something so astounding, so overwhelming that entered me to the very centre of my being. That's all I can tell you.

I was so moved that I left the room in a stunned state. In the courtyard there was a bicycle lying around. I jumped on it and fled. I have no idea whatsoever how many dozens of kilometers I must have covered. Afterwards I thought to myself "You have been in the presence of God." And there you are.

Could you physically see or hear this presence ?

No. No words were uttered. I saw nothing. Nothing. But the presence was unbelievably strong. I knew with every nerve in my body that I was in the presence of God.

What happened to your usual critical faculties, which in any other situation would make you doubt your first impression, would make you check again and search out any counter-evidence ? They didn't come into play here, did they ?

I very quickly realized that I was experiencing a conversion and that indeed I should put it to the test to see if it held strong or not. So I set about reading antichristian writers. By the time I was eighteen I had read Celsus, Holbach and also Marx whom I'd come across earlier. My faith did not budge. It was for real.

At the moment that this "revelation" occurred did it cross your mind that perhaps your senses were playing tricks on you ?

No. I was in excellent shape both physically and psychologically. I was well-balanced. Of course I did entertain that possiblilty but finally I rejected it.

Have you ever felt like writing about your conversion and how it happened ?

Chapter 5

I have never written about it and have no intention of ever doing so [2]. Once again, I don't like talking about myself. As I have already explained for my poems, they give away too much about me. And I certainly wouldn't like to behave like a second Claudel. After all my conversion is a matter between me and God and it really isn't anyone else's business.

Perhaps it's because you are afraid of ridicule that you don't want to ?

Don't worry on that score. I've never been in the least afraid of ridicule.

From your description it was sudden, violent and disturbing. There was nothing of the beatific illumination about what happened ?

Certainly not. And it didn't involve fear either but I was stunned. Meeting God had brought a complete change in my whole being. To begin with this meant a re-ordering of my ideas. I would have to think differently now that God was near me.

Following this "startling" encounter I believe your actual conversion happened at a much slower pace ?

Yes, it was a process which went on for years. On the one hand I knew that I had experienced something fundamental and unquestionable but on the other hand I wanted to avoid God's presence in my life. No doubt this has to do with my need for independence. I didn't want to have to depend on anyone in my life. What I hadn't understood was that faith can bring extraordinary freedom. For me Christianity was a sort of orthodoxy, a moral constraint and not at all a sort of liberation.

You spoke of having to re-order the way you thought. Does this mean you already had a structured mind at this stage ?

I had an academic mind. In secondary school we didn't do anything too fanciful, believe me. I had done very well in my final year, majoring in the humanities. I had studied metaphysics but that left me cold. Intellectually I was in good working order but nothing more.

Who were your favourite writers ?

First and foremost I loved Goethe. In Latin Tacitus was my favourite. Now because we were not well-off we didn't go away so during the holidays I would pass my time translating. For my own pleasure I translated both of Goethe's Fausts and Germania by Tacitus.

What attracts you to these writers ?

First of all there is a formal reason. Tacitus wrote the most beautiful Latin ever, with an astonishing density of ideas. He was able to say the maximum with the minimum of words. What drew me to Goethe was above all the poetic beauty of his work and also a depth of feeling even if at a later date I was to find his second Faust superficial.

Among French writers I can say that I love Balzac and I find Stendahl boring. I enjoyed reading *Les Paysans, Le Médecin de campagne,* because of the closeness to the characters he generated. The harmony of Leconte de Lisle and Alfred de Vigny's poetry delighted me.

What about philosophy, what about Bergson ?

I was taught Bergson by a truly excellent teacher but I didn't get caught up in his ideas. The impression I had from reading Plato for example was that it was always possible to present the converse of any argument and be equally convincing. Philosophers have always struck me as people who live in another world. They exist entirely in their minds.

You came to Kierkegaard after your conversion, didn't you ?

Yes, quite some time later in fact. I was captivated by Kierkegaard because what he said went straight to my soul. Quite abruptly I realised that reasoning with the intellect alone and reasoning based on living experience are simply worlds apart. My passion for Kierkegaard began at that time and has remained with me through the rest of my life.

Subsequently you used philosphy only as a means of enriching your own approach ?

I never indulged in philosphy. Never. Whenever I heard that a philosopher was attacking something that I, personally, was convinced about I always wanted to hear what he had to say. That's all. But I never even entertained the idea that one could possibly discover something through philosophy.

Didn't you borrow the use of dialectics from Marx and Hegel ?

Dialectics involves essentially the same argumentation as that used in the Bible. I tried to demonstrate this in a little commentary I wrote on the Book of Ecclesiastes [3] where what is important is the interplace of contradictory themes. I do not hold with the commonly held view of historians that "It is impossible that one and the same man should be the author of a particular statement and the contradiction of that statement." Well I claim it is possible. Given that this intellectual exercise involves making two assertions and testing them one against the other.

Chapter 5

In a fairly recent book [4] Lucio Colletti has shown that dialectics has its limits. By pushing dialectic argumentation too far, there is a risk, surely, that you could end up engaged in sophistry ?

Dialectic reasoning is not something superficial it withstands time. It is not a matter of deciding yes or no but of determining how one thing affects the other in order to be able to pass to another level of understanding. For historians you must understand it is essential that a method contains a time component. It was for this reason that I was attracted to the work of Marx.

You discovered Marx prior to your conversion I believe ?

I read Marx after my conversion. But I first heard about Marx when I was at the university in 1929, in a tutorial given by my dear old political economics professor, Joseph Benzacar. It was of particular interest to me at that time for a reason I have mentioned earlier. My father was unemployed. I considered it was dreadfully unjust that a man of his ability should find himself in such a predicament. I was to find an explanation for the tragedy of my father in Marx's analysis of capitalism and the crises of capitalism.

Did you begin by reading the Manifesto, the Civil War in France or the Poverty of Philosophy ?

I tried reading *Capital* first and of course I had to give up. But then I read *German Ideology* and that really got to me.

During your student years did you go into Marx any more deeply ?

Yes. Eventually I read his complete works. What is more, some time previously I had discovered a movement called *Esprit* together with Bernard Charbonneau and we had studied the critical essays and ideas of Marx together.

Were you involved in politics when you were a lycée student ?

Personally I wasn't involved in politics but in my final year class for humanities majors there were some of my classmates who were members of the *Jeunesses Patriotes*. What these boys really loved best were the nationalist marches. This got my back up no end and out of revulsion sent me straight into the leftwing camp, not that I really knew what that was however. I simply did not want to be like them. This particular response was not the well-thought out one it was to become after the demonstrations which took place on Febuary the 6th 1934.

When and in what circumstances did you meet Bernard Charbonneau ?

We were together from the beginning of the secondary school onwards. He was already remarkably eccentric and untidy. I was fascinated by his brilliant mind but was rather put off by his savage wit which frightened me somewhat. He was just the opposite of me. He did not work hard, he did not do well. We had nothing in common until one day, during our freshman year at the university, he invited me to go camping with him in the Pyrénées.

There were just the two of us, entirely by ourselves in our camp up in the mountains. I was bedazzled to find myself with someone who was ten times more cultivated than myself, who could talk about loads of writers I'd never even heard of and who miraculously seemed to have found something in me that he appreciated. Perhaps it was my gravity or perhaps my ability to listen. And goodness knows Bernard needed someone to listen to him.(Laughs). After that we often went on camping holidays together and became close friends.

What did you get out of this friendship ?

Charbonneau taught me how to think and how to be a free spirit. Between the way I had been brought up by my father and the education I had received at school I had the single track mind of the good student. He got me out of this mindset and taught me how to think critically. Among other things he taught me, a confirmed city-dweller, to love nature and the countryside.

You were a self-confessed Protestant and he was rather antichristian ?

Strictly speaking Bernard could not be described as antichristian. The Protestant scouts had left a deep mark on him but from the very outset he always claimed to be an agnostic and from that he never wavered even though he was to go through some experiences which would bring him closer to Christianity.

Do you consider him as your intellectual equal ?

Today the answer is yes, but for years he was my intellectual master. He was the one who told me what to read and influenced my views on society. Make no mistake about it he was the captain and I was an excellent first-mate.

Can you explain why his work has gone unrecognized ?

As Bernard used to say "I attacked society at its most sensitive points. If you attack society, society will hit back, the weapon it uses is silence." I believe he was right.

Can you tell me more about your activities during your student days ?

I divided my time between attending classes, reading and working to keep myself. I used to give private classes every evening for a couple of hours. From 1932 or 1933 onwards much of our time was taken up with meetings of the Bordeaux section of the Friends of *Esprit*. By then Bernard was studying History at the

Chapter 5

university and we saw each other every day. We would organize camping holidays to which we would invite along fellow students we found interesting.

Were these mixed-sex camps ?

Of course.

What were your views on that matter ?

Strange as it may seem Bernard who always seemed be rather lax was very straight-laced on sexual morality and so was I. As far as I was concerned it was out of the question to have a steady relationship with a girl if I didn't intend to marry her.

Indeed, but surely nobody even thought of you as being "lax" did they ?

No. (Laughs). But then I suppose the fact that I didn't have a cent to my name was a bit of a godsend from that point of view too. While all my friends were able to treat their girlfriends to dances or take them for coffee, there wasn't the slightest chance that I could do the same. I couldn't even treat myself to such things I simply had no money. I never tried to approach a girl and indeed I never met any girls.

Didn't this make you feel frustrated ?

No. I was happy with my private life, my reading and the more time went on the more I withdrew into my books. It was my wife who got me out of that, but that was much later on.

Did you feel any antagonism towards people who were different from you, did you feel contempt for womanizers ?

Not at all. My best friend at university a young man named Léca was an incredible womanizer. He used to have a new girlfriend every three months, and that didn't shock me one bit. I was very strict with myself as far as morals went but completely openminded towards what others got up to. It was this attitude that enabled me to work with delinquency prevention clubs in later years. Léca was to become very useful to me, he was an extremely good boxer, so after 1934 when the serious fighting began he became my bodyguard.

Were the students at the law school involved in politics ?

Everyone in the law school was right-wing. Always the individualist, my immediate reaction was if they were all right-wing then I would be different I would be left-wing. And of course the strikes over Jèze were to push me in the same direction.

Jacques Ellul

Who were the ring-leaders ?

Maurice Duverger, who at that time belonged to the *Jeunesses Patriotes*, was known to be one of the key organizers of the extreme right. He was a devoted follower of Philippe Henriot whose ideas and eloquence he so admired. I had very little to do with Duverger but as it happens he lived on rue Goya, which was not far from my home, and so we would occasionally walk back from the university together. He was a most curious character. For example I discovered one day during the course of a conversation that, like me, he greatly admired Malraux. I found this most peculiar coming from him, but there again I suppose he always had been deeply eclectic.

You just mentioned the strikes over Jèze. What happened exactly ?

They happened in 1934 or 1935 shortly after Mussolini had invaded Ethiopia. Professor Gaston Jèze was defending the cause of Ethiopia before the International Court of Justice in the Hague. This provoked an incredible mobilisation of extreme right-wing students in all the law schools throughout France, who called for the resignation of Jèze on the grounds that, in their view, fascist Italy was acting within its rights.

In the turmoil I can still see myself grabbing demonstrators by their jacket lapels out of the fray and asking them "But do you have the faintest idea who Jèze is ?". They had no idea but kept on shouting "Jèze must go !". For me that was quite a revelation into the base mentality of the masses.

In the end there were only three of us left standing against these baying hounds. There was Henri Rödel, who was shot by the Germans during the war. There was a girl, who looked as if she may be Dutch and who was trying to curb the demonstrators. And there was me.

And who was the Dutch-looking girl ?

She was my future wife. We married in 1937. She was a first year law student and I was working for my doctorate. When we met she had already trained as a nurse. Her father lived in South Africa and didn't look after her at all. It was her grandfather who had decided that she wasn't strong enough to be a nurse, which was quite true. On his advice she had turned to law, but that didn't interest her at all.

Was she involved in politics ?

Strictly speaking, no. She had leanings towards the *Jeune République*[5] movement but what really disturbed her deeply was crowd behavior. It was enough for the crowd to shout against a man for her to leap at once to his defence.

Was she a Christian ?

Chapter 5

She had been an ardent Catholic. She was brought up by a former nun of an order that had been secularized who was a most admirable woman indeed, and whom I came to admire enormously later on. At about the age of eighteen she started asking herself the usual questions one asks at that age so she sought out a chaplain to help her. He listened to her very patiently with a gentle smile on his face then said : "My dear little Yvette, I've already dealt with all your questions in the catechism class. Now you just look back through what you learned and you'll find all the answers."

Yvette stood up and said "Goodbye. You won't be seeing me again." That was how she broke with Christianity as a whole, to the great sorrow of the former nun who had brought her up.

Was that in Bordeaux ?

Quite near, in Cadaujac. My mother-in-law lived in Paris. By the time I met Yvette she had become antichristian and was very much under the influence of Nieztsche. One day I had invited her to come camping with me. There were three or four of us on that trip. I used to read the Bible quietly in my corner. Now this intrigued her as she had never opened a Bible herself. She then asked me to explain certain passages to her and that is how, thanks to the Bible we became close. We would always read and discuss the Bible together from that time on.

---

[1] According to certain documents that turned up after his death this event took place on the 10th of August 1930, so he was in fact eighteen and a half.
[2] His elder son Jean did discover a documented dated 1973, entitled "Expériences spirituels" in which Ellul relates this experience.
[3] *La Raison d'être. Méditation sur l'Ecclésiaste.*
[4] *Tramonto dell'ideologia*, Laterza, Roma-Bari, 1980.
[5] The *Jeune République* league succeeded to Marc Sangier's "Sillon". It was founded at the outbreak of the First World War and situated on the Left-wing of social-catholicism.

CHAPTER SIX

Personalism. The Hitler Youth. The Wandervogel. Scout and anti-scout. Bernard Charbonneau. Camps in the Pyrénées. Cult of effort or of pleasure ? At a Nazi meeting. Esprit. Emmanuel Mounier. Pioneers of ecology. The Bordeaux branch of the Friends of Esprit. Letter to Hitler. The third way. Ordre Nouveau. Non-conformists. "Think globally, act locally." The civil war. The power of ideas. Anarchists. Georges Bataille. The Uriage School.

Patrick CHASTENET - *What are your views concerning the allegation that there is a certain Pétainist, even fascist, ideology within the personalist movement ?*

JACQUES ELLUL.- I consider the idea that that could be so as a very bad joke. It was perfectly possible to be anti-communist and anti-capitalist and in search of a third way totally the opposite of fascism and the Vichy regime.

I don't want to quote out of context but one cannot help being surprised to read Mounier using expressions like : "our fascist friends" think that... One rather gets the impression that this non-conformist "camaraderie" encompasses all the youth movements, including the more questionable ones.

Exactly. It is certain that we found certain positions taken by the early *Hitlerjugend* a priori to our liking. (Laughs). We also felt very close to the *Wandervogel* at the outset. Later on Chabonneau and I felt very uncomfortable about organizing camps in the mountains for the very reason that they could be considered as being like the *Wandervogel*. We even considered revising our pedagogical methods because of that.

Around 1930 when you organized your first camping expeditions in the Pyrénées were you actually unaware of the Wandervogel *which after all had been in existence for some time ?*

Completely unaware. Our goal was simply to get closer to nature and to enable young city-dwellers to come and live in the countryside. This corresponded deep-down to what we were and to our own experience.

Wasn't there something of a initiation rite in what you were doing which could be compared with the ideology of those German youth movements ?

No, we did not share the same ideology. But it is true that we required anyone who wished to take part in our camping expeditions to be able to spend a weekend alone in the mountains. No-one actually did that however ! As for the rite of diving into ice-cold water, that was something we had already been doing for a long time, from the time of the Protestant post-scout movement in fact. We took those scouts who were able to stand an extremely tough existence. Among other things they had to go though there was the what we idiotically called "the drawing of lots" every morning which involved diving completely naked into one of the lakes in the Vosges.

Were you all around the same age ?

Paulo Breitmayer was the eldest. Then there were two or three boys of my age, that is to say less than twenty. One of those was Pierre Fouchier who was later to become a remarkable pastor. We were the organizers of this movement which was supposed to be anti-boyscout. We would perform some of the scout rituals backwards. For us the scouts were far too disciplined and far too likely to become a youth movement in the service of the State. Whereas what we were proposing was totally anarchistic. I can still remember some of the things we got up to at night that were extremely funny.

Can you give me an example ?

Certainly. Two or three of us would decide to create havoc thoughout the camp. We would start by pulling up all the tent pegs so that the tents collapsed on their sleeping inhabitants.

Was this a Protestant scout movement ?

No it was rather a Protestant anti-scout movement. (Laughs)

Did you have a uniform ?

Absolutely not. The scouts made a ritual of raising the flag. So we performed a mock ceremony for the lowering of the flag.

Did Bernard Charbonneau come along with you ?

No. He had once been a scout but after that he refused to let himself be dragooned into any organized group whatsoever.

So at the same time as you were attending the anti-scout camps and you were also attending those of Bernard Charbonneau. Did he attach any importance to tests of endurance ?

He didn't devise endurance tests specifically. Our endurance was tested by the activities we indulged in. For instance we would walk twenty-five kilometers through the mountains because we wanted to get to such and such place.

Chapter 6

So this was in no way linked to a belief in physical effort or a glorification of virile strength ?

Not at all. Not at all. Absolutely not. We never ever held that kind of belief. Charbonneau was always saying to anyone who would listen to him that he did whatever he pleased. Of course this quest for what pleased him could entail the most incredible marches through snow-flows high up in the mountains.

I believe you attended a Nazi meeting in the thirties. Is that right ?

Yes, I went to Germany for the first time in 1934. I went again in 1935 when I attended a Nazi gathering in Munich.

Had this any connection with your activities in the personalist groups ?

Not at all I had been invited to Germany by some Protestant associations.

So how did you wind up attending a Nazi meeting ?

I went out of curiosity. There were such meetings taking place all over at that time, you know.

Did these meetings give you food for thought for your later work on propaganda ?

Absolutely. It was fascinating to see how easily a crowd could be whipped up and welded into a single unit... No-one, absolutely no-one, had any individual reactions left.

What about you ? Did you get caught up in the crowd reaction at that instant ?

No, but it was difficult not to raise my arm in the general salute. We did get lots of funny looks but somehow managed to contain ourselves nevertheless.

I thought that it was the events of the 6th of February 1934 that caused you to get involved in politics ? But in fact your involvement stems back further than that ?

Yes we were so affected by the nazis that we sought to create a movement that would be both anti-communist and anti-fascist. I can still remember it well. We went "up" to Paris for a meeting with the people who worked with Mounier. Charbonneau was rather reluctant to go because of the connotations to the word *"esprit"* which denotes both mind and spirit. He did not like that woolly term which, to his ear had a ring of spiritualism to it. As the most important positions taken by the review corresponded to our expectations we ended up by joining.

You wrote your first article [1] in Esprit in 1937 but you were active in the movement for quite some time before that ?

Yes. We had contacted Mounier about a year before the movement [2] was set up.

The first issue of Esprit came out in October 1932. I believe you met with the people running the movement about the middle of 1933. So why is there no trace of a Bordeaux correspondant before Febuary 1936 in the issue number 17 ?

First and foremost because Charbonneau never wanted to owe allegiance to anyone. He did not want the group, that we had brought together, to be described as an "*Esprit* group". After that there is the fact that Mounier did not like the idea of having provincial groups. He wanted to pull all the strings from Paris which meant that there was a certain amount of wavering about going on.

From a glance at the list of correspondants listed in each issue of the review it is not clear who actually founded the first Esprit *society in Bordeaux. Was it Charbonneau or Imberti ?*

There is no doubt that it was Charbonneau. Imberti was the founder in name only, practically he never did a thing. He never ran the society. He was an esthete and saw *Esprit* as a spiritualistic endeavour in other words exactly what we did not want. When we tried to set up a different group from his he refused to co-operate with us. I should also add that Charbonneau was extremely exclusive.

The first appearance of a report of activities concerning Bordeaux goes back to the number 21 issue dated 1st June 1934. In this report we find that your group wanted to encourage encounters between regions and was working on the federal question in the following vein- "to maintain man in contact with his neighbours and with a world where the only creative force comes from real life (....)". Is that Charbonneau speaking there ?

Exactly.

Was there already an ecologist current in the Esprit group or were you lone pioneers ?

Bernard and I were alone in advocating this particular political stance which later became the ecology movement. On the human level Bernard defended the position of the country people, the relation between man and nature and I addressed the economic consequences of emptying the countryside which I considered would be catastrophic. I clearly recall a discussion I had with Alfred

Chapter 6

Sauvy who was explaining, with a certain amount of pride, that only 4% of the peasant population was necessary to cultivate the whole of France. I was unable to stop myself from asking him what he had in mind for the remaining 96%. He couldn't come up with an answer. So I told him : "They'll all move to the towns and cities where they'll join the ranks of the unemployed."

In what you've written you've always insisted on how important it is to stay in tune with what you call the "real milieu", yet in Bordeaux, Pau and Bayonne you mainly drew people from university circles, didn't you ?

It's obvious that that was the milieu that we were able to reach. All in all throughout the whole of the South-West we were never able to get a membership of more than eighty or so people of whom twenty were based in Bordeaux.

I believe that Esprit never had more than one thousand subscribers in the thirties... In fact you were already in a minority in a minority movement.

Absolutely. You have found the right formula, in a minority in a minority movement. That's quite right.

In the period 1936 to 1937, Charbonneau and you gave a series of conferences on the technicalization of society which were published in the Journal du Groupe de Bordeaux des amis d'Esprit. *Had you already read Lewis Mumford's* Technics and Civilization *which came out in 1932 ?*

No, absolutely not. When I wrote my first book on the technological society I was unaware of Mumford's work.

What about Aldous Huxley's Brave New World *which came out in English in 1932 ?*

Oh yes. We read that at the time of its publication and "Point Counterpoint" which came out a few years later.

Did you read Arnaud Dandieu's article "Work versus man" and Alexandre Marc's "The machine versus the proletariat" both of which appeared in the July 1933 issue of Esprit ?

Obviously I did. All that fit perfectly into our perspective of challenging the machine. Goodness knows how many articles I must have written on that subject in our little review.

When the famous "Letter to Hitler" was published in November 1933, the people at Esprit *had reproached the* Ordre nouveau *for their indulgence towards national-socialism. Your quest for a third way was also open to a certain amount of ambiguity, wasn't it ?*

Our quest for a third way between communism and capitalism was our hobby-horse for many a long year. The search for this path would entail putting the Nation State in question and turning our backs on centralized parties. Hence the exact opposite of fascism.

Did you have any contacts among the people running Ordre Nouveau *?*

I had already come across Denis de Rougemont when he had come to Bordeaux to speak at the Protestant club. We hit it off from the word go, both intellectually and spiritually. And then together with Bernard I met Alexandre Marc and other members of that movement. Bernard was a little wary of the authoritarian and right-wing leanings of the review, whereas I was much more at home with *Ordre Nouveau* than with *Esprit*. Possibly because there were more Protestants there...

Do you think that this wish for a dialogue between different ideologies, from anarchism to nazism, that one finds in all these reviews may be at the root of the debate over the ambiguity of these movements in the thirties ?

Yes. Precisely one of the things that distinguished us from certain positions taken by *Esprit* and *Ordre nouveau* was our very firm attitude concerning communism and fascism. We considered that it was impossible to engage in a real dialogue with someone who was locked into a totalitarian ideology.

On the 1st of January 1935 Bernard Charbonneau took over from Jean Imberti as the Bordeaux correspondant of Esprit. One year later Charbonneau moved to Bayonne and was replaced by Jean Gouin. He was a Catholic trades-unionist....

He was very nice but an extremely weak personality. He never did anything much. Anyway I was always there behind him as a sort of eminence grise. We didn't get on particularly well.

Jean Gouin was to remain as the Bordeaux correspondant of Esprit for that year and from the 1st of January to the 31st of December 1937 you appear as the new official correspondant on the list published in the review. How did the change-over go between you ?

All that came as a great surprise to me because I was working as a senior lecturer in Montpellier at that time.

I believe you worked in Montpellier during the academic year 1937-1938 but that the previous year you were still in Bordeaux. Does that date, December 1937, mark your break with Esprit *?*

Chapter 6

Yes. Charbonneau and I had sent in our resignations to Mounier some time before the *Esprit* congress which took place at the end of July 1937 in Jouy-en-Josas near Paris. We had failed to make anything out of *Esprit* other than simply a review for intellectuals. We wanted to create a real revolutionary movement, made up of small groups of fifteen persons or so. The groups would be federated together and would be able to act locally in a concrete fashion according to the slogan "Think globally act locally."

Talking of entering into the fray, did the personalist groups in the South-West go to the help of the Spanish Republicans ?

Not at all. The personalist groups were mainly made up of intellectuals who were not inclined to physical commitment. That is what disappointed us so much in fact. Even trying to establish a community or something on those lines would be bound to fail. Charbonneau was furious to see that the movement remained essentially a Parisian movement and I was furious to see that the movement was involved in nothing concrete.

But surely this was a propitious time for action ?

Indeed it was. There was a possibility that we could have become actively involved had it not been for the example set by Charbonneau. He hated action. He would encourage the young members to reflect on matters and not at all to commit themselves to action.

What role did you play during the Spanish Civil War ?

I played a very modest role. My wife knew a certain number of young Spanish anarchists who came to France in search of weapons. I tried to get some for them through an old school friend.

So you didn't go off to fight in Spain ?

No I didn't and there are several reasons for that. The main one was that I had just met the young woman who was to become my wife and I had no wish whatsoever to leave her.

In addition to this decisive meeting there was always the problem of violence...

Exactly. What bothered me the most was the conflict between communists and anarchists. The Spanish anarchists turned out to be every bit as violent as their enemies. They didn't use anything other than bombs in their struggle for power.

But this was war...

Obviously they couldn't do otherwise short of offering themselves like lambs to be slaughtered.

It is always very difficult to imagine History as it might have been. However had you not met your future wife at that time do you think you would have felt able to pick up a rifle and go off to Spain?

I never much liked that perspective.(Laughs) But I think it was the one time in my life that I was sufficiently motivated to commit an act of violence.

Did your friend Charbonneau get himself involved in the war in Spain?

Not at all. He didn't get involved in the Resistance either always using the same argument that "To fight for one type of State against another type of State still leaves you with a State. This war between France and Germany is no business of mine."

Charbonneau would criticize *Esprit* for being nothing more than a debating society yet he himself was completely allergic to taking action and to any form of organization.

What we wanted to put into practice was a sort of anarchist ideology, we absolutely did not want to set up a party with a leader and pyramidal hierarchy. We sought to keep our members aware that they must act as individuals able to express their own ideas, and not simply to reproduce the ideas expounded in *Esprit* by Charbonneau or Ellul. We were constantly preoccupied by this. It was to turn out to be our stumbling block. We had managed to attract disciples who were loyal, faithful and true but we didn't want faithful disciples.

Would you say your venture was doomed to failure because of the traditional centralization of all things in France or because of the differences you had with Mounier?

Mounier couldn't stand Bernard's assurance. For example at a congress Bernard's word would command so much authority that he was able to gather the groups to his side which is something Mounier could never do. I would say Mounier was jealous of Charbonneau and was suspicious of me because I was a Protestant. In the end he pushed us out onto the sidelines.

For my part I found his dogmatic catholicism difficult to handle. He was a hard-line Catholic, and not at all the open-minded Catholic he tried to appear in the review. He was a Jesuit in the worst sense of the term. Insidiously he would try to bring everything round to his catholicism. I responded as a "Prot" and Denis de Rougement did the same. I criticized Mounier and the Catholics for being too optimistic, for believing that it was possible to change our society using ideas alone.

Because you yourself don't believe in the power of ideas, is that it?

Chapter 6

I believe in a rigorous analysis of the facts, in the possibility of a partial prediction of future events based on an understandng of the past but not at all in the power of ideas.

In April 1937 Mounier was to write that within the labour movement the closest ideology to anarchism was personalism....

Yes. But Mounier was hardly what you could call an anarchist. Anarchism was the opposite of his whole being.

But how many anarchist leaders have there been who have not also been authoritarian ? And what about Charbonneau ?

He never bothered to be explicitly authoritarian, nevertheless by his manner and the way he spoke he managed to exclude all those who did not go along with his ideas. On the other hand Bernard was to be more indulgent and more flexible than I ever was towards Georges Bataille, Pierre Prévost [3] and Claude Chevalley who in my eyes represented a certain type of Parisian intelligentsia that I had absolutely no time for. He was always mentioning the fact.

In the continuation of your association with the personalists did you have any contact with the Uriage School [4] ?

None whatsoever.

---

[1] *"Le fascisme, fils du libéralisme"*. (Fascism child of liberalism)
[2] The Esprit movement was set up in August 1932.
[3] Last published work : *René Guénon/Georges Bataille*
[4] The Uriage managerial college was set up in July 1940 by Captain Dunoyer de Ségonzac. It was situated just outside Grenoble and was intended to provide the intellectual and physical training for those who would be in charge of the *Chantiers* (work sites) and the various youth movements which were necessirly under the control of the Vichy régime. The personalist doctrine was the most frequently exposed during these training courses. At the outset the colleges' staff were loyal to the Maréchal but gradually moved towards the Resistance until finaly they joined the Vercors maquis.

CHAPTER SEVEN

Roman law. The perpetual edict. University career. The *Manicipium.* The *agrégation..* Senior lecturer in Strasbourg. Struck off by Vichy. The Gergovian plateau. De Lattre de Tassigny. Back to Bordeaux. Professor on the land. First potato harvest. University's independence. Henri Vizioz. Roger Bonnard. The Resistance. Violence. The National Council for the Resistance. The purge.

PATRICK CHASTENET - *How and in what conditions did you obtain your* agrégation *to be a Professor of Roman law ?*

JACQUES ELLUL - I had always had a passion for History, I was good at Latin, I was bored stiff by Civil law, I wasn't interested in Constitutional law and I didn't find Political Economics very exciting at least the way it was taught to us then. So this left me with Roman law. One advantage was that it plunged me back into Antiquity, into the atmosphere of Rome that I'd always liked and the other advantage was that I completely fell for the logical rigour of the construction of Roman law.

The method used by the Roman jurisconsults allowed for a constant adaptation of the law to fit the politico-economic situation of the day. Whereas we live in the hold of fixed legal code, the Napoleonic Code written in 1804. From a historian's point of view I found the possibility of being able to change those things that didn't work well in the law absolutely prodigious. This was done in Roman law, year after year, using a system called the *perpetual edict*.

Would you explain this system, please ?

Each year a number of texts, written in red, would be put up in the Forum by the praetor (a judge).These texts laid down the rules by which he would judge such and such case if it were brought before him. These rules were added to from year to year. Those rules that had led to fair trials or served to keep the peace in previous years were kept and with each new situation the rules were added to or withdrawn according to what was appropriate.

The praetors were always very conscientious and this system survived for over four centuries. In the end they had a huge number of texts which were known as the *perpetual edict*, since it was possible to resolve all legal problems using it. This system seems to me a thousand times more concrete and closer to real life situations than our legal system.

What made you choose a career in the University ?

Jacques Ellul

I had promised my father that if I went into law I would go on to the bitter end. Though what that bitter end entailed was not entirely clear to me. I didn't want to be a judge. Since I had no real talent as an orator there was no point in trying to be a lawyer to plead before the courts. I could not become a lawyer in private practice because I did not have the money to buy myself a practice. So the choice left to me was to take the competitive examination to be recruited into University teaching - the *agrégation*.. Indeed this profession was ideally suited to me as it left me time to get on with my own work and also to take holidays.

What you discovered in Roman law was a proportionateness between the method and the subject. Why do you always need to stick to problems involving the real world rather than addressing more scholarly questions ? Has this got anything to do with your religious beliefs ?

I've never thought about that. I've always tried to lead my life in tune with reality, apart from religious considerations. This attitude was re-inforced by my contact with Charbonneau who was able to make a synthesis of the real from material I provided. We didn't apply philosophical principles to a lesser world, our starting point was the concrete and from there we developed our ideas towards generality.

Did your teachers encourage you ?

Very much so. Roman law was a core subject which was taught from first year and I managed to win the first prize in the end of year competition. In second year I did the same thing. After that I went on to get my degree followed by one post-graduate diploma in political economics and another in public law. In 1936 I received my doctorate in Roman law.

I believe the subject of you thesis was the Mancipium. *What is that exactly ?*

The *Mancipium* was an institution found in very ancient Rome, which concerned the father's right to sell his son. But the son did not become the slave of the person who bought him. He had a very particular status, because no Roman could be the slave of another Roman. The boy's father could sell him three times over, but after the third sale the son became free of his father's guardianship and thence became a free citizen. I studied the origin and evolution of this institution which disappeared in the second century B.C.

The choice of a thesis topic is never a gratuitous one.

My Professor of Roman law who had taken a liking to me pointed me towards this subject which at that time had not be researched.

Chapter 7

Roman law represented something more for you than just a subject that you studied at university ?

Yes indeed I saw Roman law as a model on which to create a body of law, it disappeared when the emperors started making legislation by edicts and decrees.

Which year did you present yourself for the agrégation *?*

I tried for the exam in 1937, at that time it was unheard of to be accepted the first time round. I was well-placed among the "near misses". The president of the examination jury assured me that I could count on being accepted the next time. The exam took place every two years and two years later we were at war. After my near miss I was appointed as senior lecturer in Montpellier for one year, as there wasn't a job going in Bordeaux. In 1938 I was sent to Strasbourg and in 1940 I was removed from my job.

What for ?

The Strasbourg Law School had retreated to Clermont-Ferrand. When the government collapsed the Strasbourg students got into a terrible panic. I had just come out of a Faculty meeting when some students I happened to know personally came up to ask me what I thought of the situation. Quite spontaneously I told them that the last thing they should do was to go back home to Alsace because if they did so they ran the risk of being enlisted into the German army. Then one of them asked me if we could have confidence in Maréchal Pétain. I replied that we could not, certainly not. That's all. Then I went off.

A few days later I was called in to the police station. I had the good fortune to be interviewed by a delightful police captain who was clearly unhappy about having to inform me that he had been instructed to open an inquiry into the reasons for my subversive outburst concerning the Maréchal. He asked to see my identity card, at that time it wasn't compulsory to have your card on you and as it happened I didn't have mine. He coped with this by saying : "Just to be on the safe side I'll make out a new identity card for you. You'll be able to use it when you have dealings with the authorities." And that is how I got my first very own officially-forged identity card with a whole load of the official stamps on it.

The inquiry did not stop however and they were to uncover the fact that my father was English. Now anyone with a foreign parent was not considered suitable material to work on government service so I was removed from my post in July 1940.

Did your wife go with you to Clermont ?

Yes. By then we had our son Jean as well.The place we found was south of Clermont at the base of the Gergovien plateau. We hated city life so we rented an abandoned presbytery in a delightful little village there. Every day I would walk three kilometers to the University and three kilometers back. One day at the time of the government's collapse who should turn up, amid a roll of drums, but de Lattre de Tassigny and his division with the intention of making the plateau a center of resistance. He sent a messanger to inform us that they would be needing our presbytery and that we should move out as soon as possible. I was rather put out about this so I went to see him to explain our situtation. He was very kind and asked where I would like to go. I explained that I had nothing more to do there and that I would very much like to get back to Bordeaux. He provided a military car, a chauffeur and passes. And that is how we got back to Bordeaux.

And what happened when you got there ?

There wasn't enough room for us with my parents so we settled in Cadaujac for a few months in the house of the woman who had brought up my wife. I was in a very difficult situation because, not only did I not have a penny to my name, according to the terms of my dismissal notice I was supposed to re-imburse all the money that I had been paid since the 1st of January 1940. Fortunately no-one ever came after me for this money. After that I was very lucky in what happened. The Dean in Strasbourg, an admirable man called Delpech, had managed, and goodness knows how, to pay me my senior lecturer's salary for four months. This helped to tide us over nicely for a while.

The second stroke of luck came when, quite by chance, I learned that the French Académie was offering a prize for a work on the following subject : the comparative study of recruitment into the French army in the sixteenth and seventeenth centuries. I had nothing better to do so I had a crack at it and I won. So the Académie awarded me the equivalent of twenty thousand francs in today's money. This was well paid indeed and served to tide us over even longer. Next some friends lent us their property in the Entre-deux-Mers where we settled in to live like peasants.

I believe this was a very important episode for you, am I right ?

I shall always remember how wonderfully we were welcomed in Martres. When we arrived in the village of five hundred inhabitants we were like refugees, we had no resources whatsoever. I knew nothing about agriculture and we had more than a hectare to be worked. Our neighbours taught us everything with the utmost of kindness. Several of them got together to clear the ground of weeds and undergrowth and then I set too and turned the soil with a spade. They taught me the right time to plant. I grew corn for my wife's hens and vegetables for our daily needs. I've often told my students that I felt much prouder when I brought in my first crop of potatoes than I ever did when I won a place as a University professor.

You had made the best of things and paradoxically perhaps you derived a certain pleasure from playing the intellectual on the land ?

It was Charbonneau who had first introduced me to the pleasures of nature. And indeed this experience, which lasted right up to the Liberation, turned out to be

Chapter 7

rather agreeable. Especially for my wife who had green fingers. During this time, deep down in the country, I was studying hard to take the *agrégation*. At the time of the 1941 exam I was informed that I was disqualified from taking part because I had been dismissed from my job. A friend called Chavenon, who was a senior member of the Council of State, encouraged me to lodge an appeal against this measure. The appeal was granted so I was able to take part in the *agrégation* in 1943. And I got in.

Did anyone bring any pressure to bear in one way or another ?

There was apparently a note in my file, though I never saw it, in Laval's handwriting which read as follows "this government servant must never be re-incorporated." The examination board presided by Olivier Martin, a professed monarchist, was made up of a majority of right-wing Catholics like Le Bras. On my way to see the results in the Paris Law School I met the president of the examination board coming down the stairs towards me with his hand outstretched. In gravelly tones he said to me "My dear colleague, I am very happy to inform you that you are second on the list and I congratulate you in spite of everything."

In other words the examination board, for all it was presided by a monarchist and made up of right-wingers, had awarded a place to a candidate who had been removed from his post by Vichy and who anyway was banned from teaching were he to succeed. You must admit this is a fine example of the independence of the university body, when it exists !

So I went back home with my *agrégation* in my pocket but I was still not allowed to take up a teaching post. This was a very embarassing situation for the people in charge at the university. One of whom, a man called Henri Vizioz did allow me to teach, clandestinely, on the basic legal studies course for two years. He was a brilliant professor of civil procedure. Very fortunately he befriended me. One day the Germans sent round a circular ordering the teaching staff to sign on their honour that they were neither Jewish nor foreign. Henri Vizioz, who was vice-Dean at the time ordered the staff not to sign and the document was sent back to the Germans with nothing on it.

Which members of the university staff resisted in any way ?

None of them. Vizioz was a right-wing Catholic and had been a Secretary of State under Vichy for a while before handing in his notice in disgust when the anti-Jewish laws were passed. As far as Roger Bonnard, the Dean, was concerned despite his great erudition and exceptional intelligence he was totally taken in by Nazi ideology. He was completely obsessed by the general orientation of the German right. He was a man of honour, I had a lot of respect for him and I believe that it was in good faith that he went off on the wrong track. He died at the Liberation [1]. Officially he died of natural causes but it is possible that he committed suicide.

What did you actually do in the Resistance ?

I was never involved in any fighting. Basically I did relief and liaison work. We were able to help a good number of Jewish families from our area. We also worked with friends from Poitiers who redirected "deliveries" from Paris to us from time to time. Despite being very run down our home was very large so we were able to house anyone who turned up : French resistance-workers, escaping Spaniards and even three Russian refugees from prison camps in Germany.

These three guys had crossed the whole of Germany and the whole of France and it was my job to get them into fit condition. They were as nice as could be. It brings a lump to my throat when I remember our first evening meal together. My wife had served them soup and invited them to start. All three of them had their heads bowed and their hands joined. They only began their meal when they had finished grace and crossed themselves with a flourish. This had me flabbergasted I can tell you. These were members of the Komsomol ! We got on extremely well together all the time they stayed with us the only thing that bothered us was their complete lack of sense of danger. They were tall and blond so they were recognizable from miles away and these silly fools roamed all over the place.

The reason we had so many people coming through our house was that it was situated only a few hundred meters from the demarcation line. I spent most of my time helping people get across into the free French zone. I was in cahoots with an organization that dealt in forged papers. So I was able to provide a whole series of people with forged identity cards or forged ration books.

I was also in contact with three neighbouring maquis in Pellegrue, Frontenac and Sauveterre-de-Guyenne and was able to transmit messages from one to the others.

So you were a go-between, in fact ?

Yes I was. I was there to warn them of any danger as well. One day a German motorized company came and camped for a while in our garden. When I saw them preparing to head off towards Pellegrue I leapt on my bike. Since I knew all the side roads I managed to get to the maquisards to warn them just in time.

Was anyone aware of your clandestine activities ?

Yes. Of course. Whenever the gendarmes came to make inquiries about us the mayor would always answer : "No you've got nothing to worry about with the Elluls. I've got nothing on them. They are O.K." And nothing more came of it. Now the mayor was a wily old peasant. He knew perfectly well what we were up to but always covered for us. I never talked to anyone in the village about things but everybody knew. Moreover just before the Germans began their retreat some of the older inhabitants of Martres came to see me to offer their services. Their rifles dated back to the first world war but they wanted to join the fray.

Was it because of your convictions about non-violence that you didn't take up arms ?

Chapter 7

I didn't have a theoretical position on the subject. At the end of 1943 I had brought several young people to live with us who were coming to the end of their studies. We came to the conclusion that it would be better if we were armed. I got in contact with the network that provided forged documents but was never able to track down any weapons. That's all there is to it. Had we been able to lay hands on some revolvers or tommy-guns no doubt we would have joined the maquis in Sauveterre. I was perfectly well aware that if I got involved in the fighting I would be crossing over into the realm of necessity but if I had to I was quite prepared to give up my liberty.

Did you work on the elaboration of the programme of the National Council of the Resistance ?

Some time before war broke out Charbonneau and I had written a certain number of documents on the necessity of setting up a federal State and directing the economy towards what would later be called self-management. I simply sent these documents off to Henri Frenay whom I had known in Strasbourg.

In fact Jacques Ellul the Resistance worker was to the University what Jacques Chaban Delmas was to the Bordeaux City Hall : some-one who by their presence cleanses the institution of its collaborationist past and clears its reputation ?

(Sighs) I sat on the committee which purged the teaching profession and it is true I did "cover up" or more exactly I did try to play down the importance of the convictions of certain of my colleagues. We did sanction a professor of medecin who on several occasions had told his students : "You must not follow the Maréchal with your eyes closed you must follow him even if your eyes are gouged out." The rest of them had either lived out the war in cautious non-involvement or we simply didn't have enough evidence against them. I can safely state however that no-one was shot in Bordeaux without being judged.

Was it because you are a Christian that you wanted to limit the excesses of the purge ?

The most serious cases brought before us concerned infant school teachers who had slept with Germans. In fact nine out of ten denunciations were of this kind. Obviously you understand we had good reasons for dismissing these cases. Nevertheless we did sanction three high school teachers who had been outright collaborators. They were struck off from the profession.

---

[1] In fact he died in January 1944.

CHAPTER EIGHT

Bordeaux interim city council. Political parties. A prefect. Christianity and power. Serve and not dominate. A wife's influence. The comedy of power. A deanship. Post war purge. The National Liberation Movement. Elections. A systematic non-voter. The democratic game. Direct democracy. Village life during the Occupation. Mass society. Camping with Charbonneau. Mayor of Pessac.

Patrick CHASTENET - *You were delegated as a municipal councillor on the interim city council in Bordeaux from August 1944 until April 1945. Why weren't you a candidate in the 1945 elections ?*

Jacques ELLUL - I did take part in the election meetings in order to support the outgoing mayor, the socialist Fernand Audeguil. In fact the short time that I had spent in the mayor's office had given me sufficient insight into just how little power I actually had to do anything and was more than enough to decide me that a career in politics was not my cup of tea.

By consulting the archives I noticed that you skipped about every other council meeting. Why this absenteeism ?

On the one hand I was quite disillusioned, disgusted even, to see how weak our power was and on the other hand by the enormous gap that existed between the responsibilities that we took on and our actual knowledge of the dossiers. Other than that, I really had the impression that for the council meetings everything had been prepared beforehand. We merely rubber stamped what a small committee had already decided before the meeting.

Decided in a private meeting ?

Yes, exactly.

And in this private meeting didn't you ever manage to impose your point of view ?

No, not at all. The radicals and the socialists took every decision in line with their party interests. As for me, I was completely against all that. I had the awful impression that in some meetings I was no more than the partition screen.

I will name no names, but I can still see myself coming out of the city hall with an important councillor, his hand on my shoulder etc. And I said to myself :

"So that's how it works. I'm the honest chap who is there to act as a front in all these dealings".

You served as a moral guarantee ?

Exactly. And I didn't feel any vocation for this role.

Did you ever explain to your colleagues why you boycotted so many council meetings ?

Yes, I often discussed this, even personally with Audeguil. Of course, all declared their own good faith and assured me that the city hall was completely independent. As for me, I saw that things were otherwise.

Was it the lack of your colleagues' autonomy vis-a-vis the political parties that shocked you, or the shady financial practices ?

On the financial front I never noticed anything wrong, but I didn't see everything. It was mainly the lack of autonomy that bothered me. I was also on the receiving end of my friend Charbonneau's ironic observations and taunting questions which certainly made me aware of things that I had not realized myself.

He insisted on the incompatibility between being a Christian and playing a part in these kinds of political manipulation. And my wife was of the same opinion... and anyway my being involved in politics did not please her at all.

When the proposal came up that I should be appointed *préfet* - Eugène Claudius-Petit had had the idea, as well as Gabriel Delaunay - and offered the post of *préfet in* the Nord department, my wife was ABSOLUTELY against my holding any position of authority and power.

She had her doubts about the authorities in general, or did she simply think that you were not cut out for that sort of thing ?

Her whole life, from her conversion onwards, was lived according to a rigorous and strict Christian code. This is curious because she was not a Calvinist, either by birth or by her education, but she took an uncompromising Calvin-like position. My wife would say to me : "As a Christian, you cannot hold such a post. It's completely incompatible. Christian teaching is about serving, not at all about dominating or controlling".

These moral arguments were quite hard for me because it goes without saying that I was sorely tempted to take up the post of *préfet*. I thought it should be possible to do the job in a different way, even if my time at the city council had shown me the extent to which one is a prisoner to the job and dependent on technicians. I think that I would nevertheless have accepted had it not been for my wife...

Chapter 8

After these difficult years : the Occupation, clandestine classes, life on the farm, when, at the Liberation everything had become possible again, you wanted to get things moving.

There should have been great opportunities to get things done at that point. What put me off getting involved was the fact that the former traditional parties moved back into positions of power. I found that sickening. But then my wife had been right after all. Being a Christian, however, was not about exercising power but about serving others. I felt duty-bound to present the non-authoritarian face of Christianity, and since I assert myself as a Christian whenever I can, that would obviously have been considered as a Christian undertaking in the political arena. My wife, very firmly, talked me out of that argument.

What bothered her was that you were already well-known as a Christian, because subsequently you wrote that it was quite possible to be both a general and a Christian ?

Yes, later, when I understood better what I was writing about : Christian freedom. But I also realized that this freedom was a freedom to protest but not a freedom to wield power.

Surely some authorities are absolutely necessary ? Was your wife's position based on libertarian ideas or was she simply against you being involved in political power ?

It was very systematic.

So she thought that representatives of the State were necessary but that they could not be Christian ?

According to her it was all part and parcel of opportunism and social ascension. In her view, one should not live simply to make money and the same goes for wielding power. She had chosen to be a nurse, for her that involved complete dedication to nursing the sick. What she expected of me was also a life of dedication and not a life of power.

It was therefore a mistrust of all "chiefs", especially of representative leaders ?

Exactly. My wife was also against my nomination as Dean of the Bordeaux Law School. When Poplawski died, in the fifties, I was the deputy-dean *assesseur du doyen.*. So normally I should have succeeded to the deanship. There were clans and the atmosphere was quite detestable. All the clans were in favour of my nomination. I said to myself : "When it comes to it, they're in favour of my name, but certainly not of my ideas of how to run a faculty". So, I asked them to vote on a little programme rather than on my name and they didn't accept that. I wanted to elaborate new university policies and not to act merely as a referee between two warring clans.

In your observations on "power", there is always the theme of the powerlessness of the elected representatives in the hands of the technicians as if you fear that power corrupts man. Yet during the purge at the end of the war you practically had the power of life and death over the people brought before you.

Absolutely and I always came down on the side of life. At the Liberation, I was on several juries where we had to judge a certain number of collaborators and I was always indulgent. My position was the following : as long as the enemy was active and strong, we had to do everything to defeat them. Once we had defeated the enemy we had to be as liberal as possible. We must forgive not seek revenge, nor sanction after the event when we were in a position of power and had the upper hand.

The irony of the story is that I had to judge the wine merchant, Louis Eschenauer, for economic collaboration. I actually managed to persuade the court not to sanction him as it would have liked to have done. Now I had personal reasons to be very badly-disposed towards him because he had unfairly sacked my father before the war.

You were regional secretary of the National Liberation Movement. Some observers have expressed their doubts concerning the efficiency of this movement made up of intellectuals...

Ah no. There was Henri Frenay, Gabriel Delaunay, Claudius-Petit and many others who were neither amateurs nor closet resistance fighters. Ideally the NLM intended to be a movement that completely rejected the pre-war model of political parties. We hoped that this movement would appeal to a larger audience than the traditional socialists and radicals.

Was that the aim of your personalist approach in the 1930s ?

Exactly. What I felt was important was not simply to reproduce the usual structure of bureaucratic parties but to create a real "movement". We hoped to rally people around a revolutionary, yet not at all communist programme which had been elaborated during the Resistance. I think it was a movement that could have had considerable impact unfortunately it remained embryonic.

Who did you vote for in the 1936 elections ?

I've never voted in my life.

That wipes out a dozen or so questions that I wanted to ask.

(Laughs) I've never participated in elections [1].

Chapter 8

But are you registered as a voter ?

Yes. I've got my voter's card and I receive one regularly (Laughs). I don't believe that people designated by the electoral system are up to the job. I am not putting the principle of democracy into question, but I cannot believe in a democracy founded on large scale elections.

Athenian democracy, on the other hand, was based on elections where everybody knew everybody else. Why ? Because Athens was a city the size of Pessac today. If it were a question of having real political power in a state the size of Pessac, then I would certainly commit myself to politics since I would know all the actors. But, in present day democracies an anonymous authority governs an anonymous electorate.

Alternatively is there not a risk of such a micro-society becoming totalitarian ?It could turn into a phalanstery, small units in which everybody knows each other, where each person controls the other in a permanent state of transparency and which would eventually become suffocating. Logically the next step would be the panopticon, don't you think ?

Yes, but it would be a non-objective panopticon. How many times have I heard that when talking about rural communities where everybody is watching everybody else and where everyone knows each other. Well let me tell you that never bothered my wife and me. We were always on excellent terms with the peasants in Martres. They knew that we took in many Jews, escaped prisoners and resistance fighters, but they never said a word.

Maybe you would talk differently had the experience turned out badly. More precisely I am refering to informers or to the climate of hatred and fear which was always generated whenever there were poison-pen letters ?

Maybe. But I don't really know any villages other than that one where I lived during the war and in which we only came across tremendous solidarity.

Your ideal of direct democracy would only be possible in small demographic units. Such a vision could be labelled aristocratic ? As soon as the the idea of Number or the masses appears you back away claiming...

That's not for me...

.......that's not how I play the democratic game.

It's true. My position is rather aristocratic if you mean by that that I believe in small communities rather than in mass society. I have always been against the mass society and any civilization founded on the media which is nothing but a variation of mass society. I don't believe in the wisdom of the masses.

Wouldn't you say that there was a hint of elitism in the camps you organized with Bernard Charbonneau ?

There is no doubt about that. We wanted people who would be able to live alone in the forests or mountains. I believe it is very good to train people to be able to cope with solitude and fend for themselves in the wild.

Bourdieu, on Heidegger, talks about those German students who, in the inter-war years, after having scaled up mountains would sneer on the "piles of pigs" they had left below in the valleys. The cult of the wild and of physical effort is everywhere in Nazi thinking...

Neither Charbonneau nor I ever made a cult of physical effort.(Laughs) We never shied away from hard work, we could walk for twenty-five or thirty kilometres with heavy ruck-sacks on our backs, but that was never one of the goals we set ourselves in life. We were a pair of amateurs who simply enjoyed walking in the Landes or the Spanish Pyrenees because it was such a pleasant thing to do. It was marvellous to be able to wander freely in such large open spaces.

The camps that we organized with our students were all about creating a liberating atmosphere. We wanted them to become aware of the mediocrity of the bourgeois lifestyle and we gave them a good mixture of intellectual and practical training. They went sailing with me and hiking with Bernard. We never had any intention of having a nation-wide influence. From our experience and what we achieved we were very critical of the indoctrination practised by the various national movements on their members.

Going back to the elections, since you advocate acting locally why didn't you try to become mayor of Pessac ?

That was a possibility in the elections of 1959, if my memory serves me right. A delegation of socialists and communists asked me if I would head the list in opposition to the outgoing mayor, Doctor Dalbos. I accepted on one condition that I would be free to fill a third of the list with independent personalities. They didn't like that. They wanted me to preside over a list made up solely of socialists and communists. I wouldn't back down. And neither would they.

So you weren't totally disillusioned by politics. But, once again - just like the deanship - you had set the bar impossibly high, hadn't you ?

Well there was also the rectitude of my wife to be taken into account she encouraged me never to compromise, either with evil or with opportunity, and my Protestant convictions were telling me much the same. Politics is not an easy game to play and I would have been an awkward partner. When I met someone of the callibre of Gabriel Delaunay, I was more than willing to work with them politically.

Chapter 8

Did you meet often ?

No, very rarely in fact.

Would your wife have accepted that you become mayor of Pessac ?

Maybe, as long as she felt sure that I wouldn't become a prisoner.

You say : "Never compromise in the face of Evil", doesn't that rather imply that you are in the possession of Goodness on the side of Good. With beliefs like that you could easily fall into fundamentalist behaviour without realizing what you where doing, couldn't you ?

Yes, but as Christians do believe that they are on the side of "Good". This Good is known as Love and as Freedom. If there is love and freedom no sort of fundamentalism, judgement or exclusion can exist. What I have to teach people is that Christ loves the world, therein lies their liberation so I cannot possibly be a slave and bring the message of liberation..

The fact that you are very rigourous - generally associated with a Puritan image - could be misinterpreted as intolerance perhaps ?

Yes, if my rigour became authoriarian I suppose but not if I used it to liberate others. My refusal to compromise means that I would also refuse to let others be led astray..

---

[1] He was a candidate for the October 1945 elections.

CHAPTER NINE

Places to write. Anarchists. Totalitarian States. Sources. Bernard Charbonneau. Genuine democracy. Professional politicians. The prevention club. Delinquents and community workers. Elections. Political illusion. Sociology and theology. Objectivity in the social sciences. The author and his work.

PATRICK CHASTENET.- *Where did you write most of your books ?*

JACQUES ELLUL.- Here in Le Canon, during the holidays. Throughout the year I would prepare all my documents in Bordeaux but for the actual writing I needed to be somewhere where I felt relaxed and had complete silence. I would work every morning from about half past five until eight o' clock and then I was free for the rest of the day. It took me about two and a half months to write a book which I was able to do during the summer.

We bought this house in the sixties. It was here that I wrote *Métamorphose du bourgeois, Exégèse des nouveaux lieux communs*, as well as all my books published by Calmann-Lévy and those by Seuil publications. I wrote *La Technique ou l'enjeu du siècle*, between 1948 and 1950, in the forest of La Coubre.

Amongst your sources we find constant reference to Marx and the Gospels, Kierkegaard and Barth, Charbonneau and Jean Bosc... Why are there so few references to anarchist writers ?

Towards the end of the 1930s I was an avid reader of Bakunin, Proudhon and I also read some Kropotkin. In as far as I felt the State was forever encroaching in domains that where outside its mandate, I felt that the anarchists' reponse was right, not for all time but in the actual context of modern society.

I am very close to their conception of revolution and society. But, intellectually, the anarchists have not impressed me. They gave me ideas, a certain way of thinking, but they have not "added" anything to my thinking. Unlike Marx, whose way of thinking influenced me greatly. I have read all his books and annotated everything in them, I found the anarchists' works a little superficial.

So it is not your anarchist leanings which have conditioned your critique of the State ?

No, because we based our critique of the State on what we saw happening before our very eyes during the thirties. These was the fascist State, the totalitarian State and so on, and then there was the recurring critique of the liberal State. In fact we didn't set out to make a global critique of the State. Our critique was marked by historical manifestations of the State.

So you weren't decrying the State as such ?

In the end we were. At first we criticized the fascist State, then the hitlerian State and then the communist State and then, I remember our surprise and amazement when Charbonneau and I realized that after all the American State, with its capitalistic organization could be just as totalitarian, just as authoritarian and that it sucked people into its system just as the others did. In other words, our critique was the fruit of an experimental and historical observation and not at all theoretical or abstract. It was later that we read the anarchists.

Did Charbonneau read Proudhon ?

It's very difficult to know what he had and had not read. In actual fact I believe that he was very well-read but that he never let on.

Did his "The State" influence you ?

Not at all because it brought me nothing new. We had worked on it together. I remember that we had discussed which aspects of present-day society we should deal with and Charbonneau wanted to tackle the question of the State himself. I told him that as I was the lawyer that subject was more in my domain. He wouldn't accept that and told me to look into the question of "technology". So that is how we shared out the work. We had such a communion of thought that I could have said everything he said on the State and he everything I had to say on technology. The writer who influenced us the most was Tocqueville, especially his "American Democracy".

Charbonneau's refusal to come down on one side or the other concerning Nazi Germany and the Allied forces is rather comparable to your refusal to choose between caricatures of democracy and full-blown totalitarian regimes ?

Yes, with the distinction that in the end I did make a choice.

In your life certainly, but is that true for your writing ? I am thinking of a passage in, "The Political Illusion" where you describe those people who fight to defend democracy as being fools because democracy is already dead. Isn't this a typically idealistic vision of democracy ?

It's not an idealistic vision. If the political class did not exist and if we started again from scratch, it would be perfectly feasable.

Chapter 9

Yes, but if like Ostrogorski and Schumpeter we take democracy as we actually find it and not as we believe it should be we have to admit that the regime cannot function without professional politicians.

It is obvious that true democracy can only work in micro-groups. We have always thought the nation-state should be divided up into workable provinces. Effective democracy can exist at a provincial or communal level. It's the old anarchist motto : If you want to change the world, start by changing your own neighbourhood or backyard !

Locally I believe you are very much involved in the prevention of juvenile delinquence ?

Yes indeed, this is all due to a meeting I had with Yves Charrier in 1958. He came to me asking for legal and spiritual advice. He had been working as community instructor with a public organization and he felt that very little could be achieved for maladjusted boys by keeping them in institutions. In other words, he wanted to work with young delinquants, not in an enclosed environment, but in their natural surroundings : the street. We therefore founded the Prevention Club in Pessac and I worked there with Yves until he died in 1969 as a result of a diving accident.

Concretely, what was your role ?

Basically I was an intermediary. I was a buffer between Charrier, the police, the courts and the Social Services Department who paid his salary but wanted assurances. Actually I was the local personality who was there as a sort of caution for the running of such a marginal club. At that time in France there were no more than two or three such experiments being carried out.

Do you have any direct contact with these youngsters ?

Yes, I often went to the club and they knew that I was "the boss" as they would say. I was very well received by these young people who could in fact be very violent. I never had any problems. Something quite extraordinary happened as the deviant behaviour changed pattern from bomber jackets to the beat generation to drug addicts, some of them asked Charrier if he knew of someone who could explain the Bible to them. So once a week I gave Bible classes for thirty or so misfits who I must say turned up very regularly.

Was Charrier a Christian ?

Not explicitly ! Whenever I asked him about it he would always say, "Look, I'll look after doing what has to be done and you can do the believing for me.". (Laughs) He wasn't a Christian but he behaved as a Christian should.

Jacques Ellul

I believe Yves Charrier took great personal risks, and to his cost, by physically confronting hooligans. How did he cope with drug addicts ?

Charrier had less success with the new style delinquants than with the black-leatherjacket brigade. He once said to me : "When all is said and done, what can I do ? I know a young boy who lives in the basement of a tower block in Burck. He spends all day on a mattress on the floor. There are some girls who bring him food but he does nothing, simply nothing". In other words Charrier felt he could only do something with deliquants whose delinquency took an active form. As he often explained to me : "They have bags of energy but they burn it all up in deviant behaviour. What I do is to try to get them to channel it into doing something good". With lethargic, indolent youngsters he didn't know where to start.

Has the Prevention Club survived his death ?

Yes. After his death I took over the directorship of the club which was not easy. Then I found an excellent instructor, Luc Fauconnet, who was almost the complete opposite of Charrier, but who was the sort of person who could deal with this new type of misfit. He was a man of words. And it's true that drug addicts, although they are very sluggish in behaviour, can be immensely talkative. The most difficult part, as the new director told me, was that they wanted to start talking at two in the morning.

Did you ever feel like extending your involvement with the Pessac community by taking on a more political role ?

My brief experience on the Bordeaux City Council had put me off that sort of thing for good.

In 1981 you told me that you had not in fact written several books but only ONE book, in which each separate "book" corresponded to one chapter. Does this mean ONE book for each register or compartment or that there is one book for the whole of your work ; which brings us back to the question of interconnection of your sociological works and your theological writings.

The interplay between the two is very important for me as I have always thought that there should be a dialectical relation between a sociological and theological writing. It is not possible to read one without the other.

Since you have always kept the two distinct and always refused to see them fused into a single approach - in a closed circuit thought process - to now declare that all your writing forms ONE single book surely undermines your wish to keep them separate ?

Chapter 9

(Laughs) No, because they do belong to two different registers. They are inter-related if you like. In much the same way as a negative pole and a positive pole interact and then sparks fly between them. (Laughs)

Most sociologists and political scientists consider that your analysis of the technological society was determined by your religious convictions...

That is equally valid the other way round. I studied sociology as I studied history. I was trained in a rigorous discipline which required a lot of reading and a very critical approach to the texts. It was in fact by studying the history of Roman law that I realized that our interpretation of the Bible is generally very insufficient and very superficial.

Going back to Weber's classical distinction between values and value judgements, are you sure that you manage to avoid making value judgements in your sociological works?

I know full well that it is impossible to avoid doing that. When I write I know that what I say is "me" speaking and that I cannot speak in the name of "us all". I don't believe at all in the neutrality of the social sciences. In this field objectivity is an illusion. The only precaution I do take is constantly to scrutinize what I'm writing to make sure that I am not conforming to such or such sociological or ideological factor which conditions my thought.

What do you think of the work done on the sociology of knowledge which claims to give a scientific explanation of a writer's work based on the social conditions in which the work was produced?

I wonder if it is possible to know just how many factors are involved: childhood, life with parents, etc. Where and how does one find and define these factors and how do they interact? Actually I don't believe that it is possible to come up with a correct analysis of the factors involved in the creative act.

It is however possible to define such factors as the writer's origin, the social milieu, the period in which the work was written, and to identify certain strategies...

Yes, but there will always something very personal left out. The relationship of a child with his parents is not stereotyped. It is obvious that my relationship with my father greatly influenced my thought and my existence. And how do you measure that?

Pierre Bourdieu's reply to that would be that "personal style is only the reflexion of the style of the era and the social milieu of the writer". In other words, your father was an individual example of certain social class with given values...

(Laughs) I wouldn't agree with that at all. As I have already told you, my father was a foreigner descended from a noble (though dispossessed) Serbian family, who had received a very high-powered academic education in Vienna and went from there to take up a series of very miserable jobs in trade. He was a man of immensely strong character, who never backed down over anything. He played a great role in my life, indeed he was my role model, but I could never say that he was a typical example of his family or social milieu.

CHAPTER TEN

Living fully. Listening to others. The sensitivity of a woman. The friend and the wife. Bernard Charbonneau and Yvette Ellul. The bone of contention. Mother and daughter. South Africa. Jean-Paul Sartre. Crowds. Bach versus Mozart. I have no regrets. Foreign languages. Morocco. Hassan II.

Patrick CHASTENET - *When all is said and done, what would you say has been the most significant experience in your life ?*

Jacques ELLUL - That's difficult because I would say that in fact there have been two highly significant experiences. The first being when God came to me and the second was when I met the person who was to become my wife. These have been the decisive experiences of my life.

Yes indeed but there you're talking about long-term commitments. I was actually thinking in terms of some specific punctual event.

There was one special event that happened a long time ago that had a lasting effect on me. It happened when I saw soldiers leaving for the trenches, I have already told you about that. There is another experience that marked me very deeply but no doubt you will think that it falls into the same category as my encounter with God or with my wife, it was my encounter with the sea.

If you had to sum up in a few words what your wife has brought you, apart from her love, what would you say it was ?

I think I can answer that question by quoting something she said herself. We were not yet engaged but were seeing a great deal of each other and I was preparing for the *agrégation* exam at the time when she said to me : "Do you realize that if you go on like this you'll end up being nothing more than a bookworm ?"
I replied that I couldn't really see what else there was to do, to which she replied : "But you must live your life !" I was completely baffled by that because I had no idea what living actually meant.
That is what she did for me. She helped me learn to live. This meant that I learned to relate to others. I wouldn't say that before knowing her I was completely insensitive to the simple pleasures of life, but with her I learned to appreciate and enjoy so many things. She also taught me to listen. That is something I didn't know how to do. That's absolutely true. Being a teacher by nature I was someone who talked and who didn't listen (Laughs)

Learning to listen was useful to me in my job and even more so for me as a Christian and the work I had to do there. She used to say to me, "You can't be a good Christian if you don't listen to other people. How can you help people to understand if you don't listen to their problems and questions ?"

Obviously, and I don't want this to be taken as a criticism, I had been modeling my attitudes on those of my friend Charbonneau. He was completely impervious to other people's questions too. He would air his own views without a thought for what others might think. I was rather like that when I was twenty.

So your wife was able to change your character ?

She changed my whole way of being. After that receiving people and listening to them became a very important part of my life.

When you describe her as teaching you to "appreciate things" does this mean she initiated you into the pleasures of good food for example ?

Not really, as I was already quite a gourmand. Most important of all she showed me how to enjoy the simple things in life. I knew nothing about flowers, about their fragrance... I had always had a great love of the country. I used to walk a great deal in the woods but I had never really been able to savour and enjoy the trees and everything else there. I had never been aware of the great mystery that the forest generates. She taught me how to apprehend this secret.

Isn't that something you could have learned by reading such authors as Ernst Jünger for example ?

Everything I read stayed on the intellectual level. Walking in the forest was my exercise. I did it for the pleasure of walking. It was my wife who showed me how to see and observe all the treasures of the forest.

What were your wife's interests and her tastes when you first met her ? Which of her passions did she pass on to you ?

What she passed on to me was more a certain sensitivity that she possessed than her position on different matters. She was extraordinarily sensitive to atmosphere. Sometimes when we were in a group she would pick up any feelings of unease or tensions between various people there. As for me as long as I was talking I never noticed if anything was the matter. I was completely oblivious of anything else going on.

It was very important for her that the relationships of those people around her should be free-flowing both with her and between themselves. She found it very hard to stand the roughness of exchange that had always existed with my old friends. We could be very violent in our arguments and then be the best of friends when it was over. She would defend her ideas with much more delicacy.

Chapter 10

Did she influence you in your choice of friends?

She was very intuitive, whereas I would take people as I found them without giving a thought as to what they may be like. She taught me how to see the positive side and the negative side of other people. The big problem was that Charbonneau and she could not stand each other. This was very obvious from the moment they first met at a meeting of the *Esprit* group.

One day Charbonneau said to me, "In my opinion all English girls (which she was not) are blue-stockings (which she was not). That puts me right off." And it's quite true he found it very hard to get on with Yvette. Whenever we invited him for lunch after our marriage he was always uncomfortable. He never managed to be himself in the presence of Yvette.

I'll tell your an amusing anecdote that was typical of our relationship. Bernard had just got married to a girl who was much younger than all of us and who was extremely shy. They invited us out to eat with them. We were served a superb rib steak. Without a moment's hesitation Bernard scooped the whole steak onto his plate and began eating, as calm as you like. That was the way he was!

Yvette was absolutely horrified. I was sufficiently used to his behaviour so I simply took the steak away from him and put it back on the serving-plate. He wasn't in the least bit offended by what I did. But it was little things like this that made Yvette take a dislike to him.

Does this mean that you were torn between your wife and your best friend?

I was aware of this bad feeling during the whole of our life. In fact I was entirely on my wife's side which meant that I never went camping with Charbonneau again for example.

Nevertheless you stayed friends..

Very good friends.

So you had to see him without your wife?

Not necessarily. She accepted to see him. Just let's say that things went better when she was not there.(Laughs)

Did Charbonneau ever mention his first opinion again?

He never mentioned it again. The matter was closed.

And you never tried to get him to talk about it again?

What would have been the point?

But did it distress you to watch your wife and your best friend constantly cold-shouldering each other ?

I must say Bernard's marriage made things a bit better because his wife, Henriette, got on very well with mine. For example when we lost our small son it was Henriette Charbonneau who was closest to my wife. She understood and helped Yvette more than anyone else. Henriette was as sensitive as Bernard appeared to be insensitive. I say "appeared" because he had a sensitivity all his own.

What did your wife hold against Charbonneau apart from his boorishness ?

On the one hand she reproached him with thinking and speaking without ever listening to other people and on the other she accused him of putting on an act to appear tough. Now Bernard was not a tough man even if he did his best to be crude and abrupt.

Was you wife involved in your work ? Did she read your manuscripts ? Did she make comments about them ?

She read what I wrote. She rarely made comments on the intellectual content because she felt she wasn't qualified to do so. She was completely wrong on that score. As I go through her book-shelves today I am amazed by the quality of what she read and at the annotations she wrote in the margins. She always had something to say when it came to spiritual or religious matters. She would say : "I think you have got it right here" or "this needs to be gone into more" or "you are straying from the point."

Did she introduce you to any authors ?

I can't say she did. It is only now that I'm beginning to discover what she read.

How did she react when one of your books was torn to pieces by the critics ?

For her that was one of the little things in life that it was best to leave alone. One way in which my wife did have a considerable influence on my life was to encourage me to shun success and not run after jobs which carried responsibility. As I've already told you it was because of her that I didn't become a prefect. And even though she was never particularly fond of Bordeaux she never hankered after a move to Paris.

Even though she was always extremely elegant, and amazingly at ease at receptions (thanks to her mother's upbringing) she absolutely hated the social whirl. Whenever we attended a cocktail party for a book launch at the publishing house of the Seuil or at Calmann-Lévy she managed to behave abysmally. She would make

Chapter 10

remarks to authors, whose writing she knew pretty well, which, if they weren't exactly insulting would certainly have a nasty sting to them.

In this kind of situation she would behave most unpleasantly but would carry it all off with a lovely smile. This was so ironical that the atmosphere turned stone cold. She certainly knew how to send a chill through the gathering, that's the only word for it.(Laughs)

Why did she do that ? Was she allergic to that kind of gathering ?

That's exactly it. She knew how to dance wonderfully well but she wouldn't set foot at a ball. She hated anything that smacked of superficiality in human relations.

What would you say were her main qualities ?

I would say it was her rectitude, her strictness with herself, her sensitivity. Her musical sensitivity was sometimes astounding. In fact, and this is indeed strange but she actually managed to educate me musically. I never had an ounce of music in me before that.

Who were her favourite composers ?

The musicians she loved have today become great classics but sixty years ago they weren't so well-known. Her favourites were Bach and Mozart. She didn't like Beethoven or any of the Romantics like Schumann, Schubert and so on. Her mother had been a remarkable pianist and she sang marvellously well. If she hadn't been born into such a good family (laughs) she could have become a professional musician in Belgium. She was invited to sing at the Brussels opera in the Theatre de la Monnaie which is similar to, but less prestigious than, the Scala in Milan.

Did you get on well with your mother-in-law ?

Yes. "Matchou" and I got on very,very well. And here I'm going to let you into a family secret. There was a touch of jealousy on the part of my mother-in-law. She was a very beautiful, very attractive woman who was as superficial as her daughter was deep. She got married three times and seduced everyone around her. All the men in her circle were enthralled by her. That was her whole life, she simply adored being courted. My wife could not stand that kind of behaviour, which probably accounts for why she herself was so upright. She was that way as a reaction against the way her mother lived her life.

Who was jealous of whom ?

It went both ways. My wife couldn't stand all her mother's love affairs and it was clear that my mother-in-law wanted to add me to her list of conquests. She was very much taken aback, I believe probably for the first time in her life, to come across a man who preferred her daughter to her.

Wasn't this a purely intellectual seduction or even a game ?

Not one bit of it. She really wanted to seduce me exactly as she always did with men in her circle. She was twenty-one years older than us, exactly. So basically you understand that between a man of twenty-three and a woman of forty-four....

Let's get to some less intimate questions. Sometimes it's said that the stance you have taken over South Africa has to do with the fact that your wife's family came from there, is there anything to this ?

That is amusing but altogether false. My wife had absolutely nothing to do with the South African business. We no longer had any connections in South Africa with the exception of my father-in-law who was living there until he came to live in Switzerland for medical reasons. I only ever had anything to do with him in the last two years of his life when he was living in a sanatorium. My wife was completely indifferent to what was going on in South Africa.

One gets the impression that the fuss created over what you wrote about South Africa is inversely proportional to the volume of what you actually wrote. The few lines that you wrote on Apartheid weighed much more heavily in public opinion than the three volumes of your Ethique de la Liberté. *What is more South Africa is not your speciality, is it ?*

(Laughs) Absolutely not. I once spoke about it on television and I once wrote an article on the subject where I pointed out a certain number of facts which were difficult to accept at that time. It certainly didn't go down well in 1985 to say that the South African problem could not be boiled down simply to the confrontation between the good Blacks and the evil Whites. Even today when talking about the conflict between Inkatha and the ANC people forget to point out that it not a confrontation between opposing political parties but between warring tribes. The Zulus and the Xhosas have been fighting each other ever since the seventeenth century.

In that particular article I had the misfortune to assert that when the whites arrived in 1652 there were at most 150,000 Hottentots and Bochimans in a territory that was six times the size of France and that the problems only really began when the Bantu started moving down from central and eastern Africa.

I also mentioned that the ethnic divisions ran very deep, for example the Bantus hated the Indians much more than they hated the whites. As well as that I stated that the Africans in the South African Republic had a higher standard of living than any other black population on the African continent. And I pointed out that despite the fact that Apartheid had become an intolerable regime over the last forty years at the outset it had enabled all groups including the Blacks to flourish side by side and still keep their own specificity. Once again I was misunderstood.

Chapter 10

I really would like to know what drove you to get involved in this business? You even added to your sins by speaking out over Israel.

I wrote about events in South Africa just as I would about racial conflicts in the USSR under Stalin.

Can one speak of "race" in this context?

A good number of my friends who are physiologists would say that there is no such thing as race. But in the USSR and in South Africa the people involved are not tribes but genuine ethnic groups who are different, whether you like it or not, and who hate each other just as much as the French hated the Germans in the nineteenth century.

You must have been aware of the fact that if you wanted to explain that events in South Africa were not as simple as the Manichean version given in the media you would automatically be taken for an apologist of the racist regime in Pretoria?

That was the agitator in me coming out. I felt I had to take a different stand and explain myself because absolutely everybody was adhering to the same analysis of the South African situation. Moreover there is no question that the reason that the Zulus didn't fight the Xhosas even more than they actually did was because they had the whites separating them. This is borne out by what is happening today. As soon as the whites pulled out the war began all over again.

Marcel Merle once said of you that you had "a need to annoy". Don't you pride yourself just a little in always swimming against the tide.

Yes that is true. I have always managed to go against current trends and fashions. When I reread what I wrote about Jean-Paul Sartre when he was at the height of his fame I certainly wouldn't say the same things today. Quite the contrary. I recognised his worth. I remember very well before the war reading his first book which nobody had heard of at the time and I remember how impressed I was. Later I was irritated by the craze that welled up for Sartre so I reacted against it.

How do you explain this aristocratic distain for the rest of the common herd. You never want to be where everyone else is. This smacks of elitism, doesn't it?

Yes indeed you are quite right. Intellectually speaking that is the case. However on another level I have always enjoyed going off on my own to wander around in crowded places. I used to love the amusements fair in Bordeaux when I was a child. It was still a place where you could have a good laugh and there were plenty of attractions. I had a splendid time wallowing in the crowd watching barbers pulling teeth and the likes.

It gave me enormous pleasure to be an onlooker in the middle of things. One of my favourite walks in this respect was down the commercial street rue Saint Catherine when it was at its busiest. I loved being in a place where I could observe people's expressions and speculate on the reasons for their particular attitudes.

I take it that you are not afraid of crowds and that you have no contempt for them either ?

Oh, not at all. I am however very afraid of crowds when they become polarized. The sort of thing I saw during the Hitler period at highly charged gatherings. But I was always in my absolute element in a crowd of onlookers whenever I was in Paris. I felt really alive as I watched the students spilling out of the University onto boulevard Saint-Michel ; I found it impressive.

Alone in a crowd ?

Yes. I watch, I take everything in and weigh up the atmosphere. That is always important for me. I remember one day when my wife and I were in Rome, we found ourselves in a densely crowded thorough-fare and I said to my wife : "Listen. I feel very uncomfortable I've got the feeling that there is a revival of fascism going on here."

She asked me what on earth I meant by that. So I explained : "Can't you see the way these people are greeting each other, don't you notice anything about the way they are walking? It's almost as if they are marching in step. There is nothing Roman about that, nothing Italian either." Very shortly after this I was proved right when the creation of the Italian neofascist party, the MSI, was announced.

Do you ever go and sit on the terrace of a café just to watch the crowds go by ?

Never.

I take it you wouldn't write one of your books in a café then ?

I could never do that. The only place I can write is in my office. I need absolute calm, no noise (except music) and I must not be interrupted.

But you can work to music, however ?

Yes. I even associate certain of my books with particular records. I can listen to the same piece of Bach or Mozart played thirty times over. This may strike you as rather strange but I wrote *La Technique* to the Brandenburg Concertos. I preferred listening to Mozart when I was working on my books on theology.

Chapter 10

Do you know Karl Barth's story about Bach and Mozart ? Karl Barth, who was the greatest Protestant theologian, adored Mozart. He even wrote a book about Mozart's theology. One day someone asked him : "But what about Bach ? Don't you like Bach ?" and Karl Barth replied : "But of course. Of course. I know that they are bound to play Bach for our Eternal Father at all the great ceremonies in Heaven. But they say that when the Eternal Father wants to hear the music he really enjoys he puts on Mozart in secret."

What do you regret most in your life ?

This is going to sound very pretentious but I don't really regret anything. Nothing apart from having been a little impatient with my wife towards the end of her life. Otherwise I regret nothing in my life, even if I have sinned. I'm not a saint.

I was thinking in terms of what you would have liked to have done or to have seen achieved. Or of an area which may have disappointed you ?

First of all there are books that I would have liked to have written and that I never got round to. For example I would really have liked to write a book about what the sea has meant to me. Next I regret having several hundred unfinished poems that I can't be bothered to go back to. I criticize myself for that sometimes.

So that is what you regret about writing. Are there any regrets concerning your life as a man of action or simply your life as a man ?

I don't regret much in fact. Perhaps I focused too much on myself that is true. I always succeeded what I wanted to succeed in. Perhaps I didn't help others enough. Although I do know that my students appreciated me, liked me and I helped them to the best of my ability. I don't judge myself severely even though I wasn't always what I should have been as far as my wife was concerned.

On a different level have you ever regretted not being a painter or a musician for example ?

Not at all. A painter ? My mother was a painter that was enough for one family. A musician ? I'm very fond of music but I'm tone deaf. One of my grandsons came up with a delightful comment concerning that. We had been at a service and I had sung the hymns, no worse than I usually did. As we left the church he came to me to say : "I say, Grandfather, do you think you could not sing so loudly in future. Because you sing out of tune and you bring everyone else out of tune with you." (Laughs)

I don't have a musical ear. That could be the reason why I can't speak English. I speak German and Italian fluently thanks to my father. From the age of ten or eleven he used to read aloud on Sunday afternoons. At the lycée I was always top in German and I feel really at home in Italy.

Jacques Ellul

Why did you never go to the United States, contrary to what is sometimes written about you ?

For precisely the reason that I don't speak English. The Americans are much kinder than the English from that point of view. They double up with laughter but they do try to understand what I have to say. As for the English I always have the impression of talking to a brick wall. I felt this a lot when I went to England but it was completely different in Scotland where I had no problems whatsoever.

You also spent some time in North Africa, didn't you ?

Yes, I went to North Africa several times. Mainly in Morocco. As it happens I had the future King of Morocco as a student in Bordeaux. There was an Institut Français in Rabat, the director was a friend of mine so he invited me to teach courses there quite regularly. In fact I almost became director myself had it not been for trick played by some Paris colleagues which prevented me from getting the post. I must say there was another (quite typical) incident which may have weighed against us.

When we had been in the Moroccan area of Rabat my wife had seen a little Moroccan house which she found enchanting. She made the following blunder during a very formal official dinner, I don't think she did it on purpose. Addressing the other guests she said : "Oh it's so marvellous here. If ever we are posted to Morocco I would want to live in the Arab district." If you could have seen the frozen expressions on the faces of the French people present. Imagine a French government official living in the Arab district, it was unthinkable. I'm sure that this affected my nomination.

When did that happen ?

That was in the fifties, when Morocco was still a French protectorate. I used to go there two or three times a year to give classes in History and courses on the influence of western law on the Arab world.

And what about Hassan the Second ?

I remember a little anecdote about him. When he was very young he came to take his doctorate in Bordeaux. I had to give him one of his oral exams. He was a brilliant student, had worked very hard and knew everything he was supposed to know. At the time our Dean was a man called Poplawski who was overflowing with courtesy for important people. He was very anxious about our student and came to me to ask if everything had gone well. To which I replied quite curtly : "No. Very badly. I gave him a very poor grade." The poor man was completely flustered : "But it's not possible. You can't possibly do that to the Sultan's son. Can't you see its crazy to do that ?"

So I managed to give the Dean of the Bordeaux Law School a nasty fright. And I had a good laugh afterwards as I tried to reassure him that it was only a joke.

CHAPTER ELEVEN

Freedom of man in the freedom of God. The dilemma of non-believers. The New Jerusalem. Recapitulation. The historical will of man. God is Love. The Word of God. Prophets and false prophets. Democracies and dictatorships.

Patrick CHASTENET - *What do you make of the problem that Bakunin posed : if God exists then man is a slave. Man is free, so God does not exist ?*

Jacques ELLUL - That is absurd if you consider that in the Bible God is generally described as being the *Liberator*. How does God manifest himself? By setting people free and not by condemning them. The fundamental and classical element is much less Genesis than Exodus. God is the one who sets his people free. For each one of us the knowledge of God frees us from a certain number of elements that weigh heavily on us : we are freed from destiny, freed from the anguish of living and freed from the fear of death, we are freed from our sins.......

God is not the master of the universe but the *Liberator*, Jesus Christ behaved as the *Liberator*. That is why he got into a fight with the Pharisees because they transformed God's Law - in other words the law of liberty and freedom - into sets of rules, moral codes, dogmas. Jesus swept all that aside.

Listening to you sometimes one would think that man is only truly free when he acknowledges God's freedom. Would you say that Barth was indulging in a little sophistry when he spoke of the the obedience of the free man to the free God ?

That is in fact the case, man, who is free, obeys a God, who is free. Consequently this free God could never want a slave as his counterpart. When we read of the creation of Adam in the Bible he is presented as being a counterpart of God. He is the guarantor of God's love. He is not a puppet figure.

He becomes a mere puppet from the moment that he breaks off from God. When the bond is broken the forces of evil surge up, with the forces of destiny and all the forces that go to producing a whole series of catastrophes. It is not by wishing to be free that man brings about catastrophes it is by spurning God's love that he brings all this on.

It is God's will that man be free. If Jesus died on the cross it was so that man could be free.

How do you answer the dilemma of the non-believers according to which either God is almighty and therefore bad ; or God is good and therefore powerless ?

That dilemma is based on a poor knowledge of the biblical revelations and of God. In that they show that God is almighty and that he does as he wishes, without taking anything else into account but himself. Now God shows us in his first revelation that he is a God of dialogue. Consequently he respects those with whom he dialogues. He does not constrain, he does not force set responses and that is why the Churches are always making mistakes when they devise lithurgies or present dogma purporting to be *"The"* truth.

There is no truth in the Church. Truth transpires through the multiplicity of opinions, on condition that they flow together into an adoration of the same God. But this is a God who wants man to be free. Péguy wrote prodigious things on this subject where he said more or less the following : there is no possible comparison between the adoration of a French knight as he kneels in prayer and the cowardly grovelling of an Oriental slave before his master.

If we speak of an omnipotent and hence bad God, this implies that we hold him responsible for all that is bad that occurs on earth : wars, catastrophes, epidemics etc.

Which is not true. I'll give you one example just to show how badly we can get things wrong. Take this verse from the Gospel according to Saint Luke which says : "Not even a sparrow falls to earth without it being the will of God." Now that is not the correct translation. The passage in Greek reads as follows : "Not even a sparrow falls to the earth *without God knowing*." This means that even when a little bird falls to its death God is there to accompany it at the moment of its death. It does not at all mean that God MADE IT DIE. That opposition is very important.

This distinction could be used when considering war for example ?

Exactly. War is brought about by the will of man. It is not God who starts off wars. That would be the horrible view of an almighty God who made and did everything. That doesn't correspond to the God of the Bible one bit ! The God of the Bible gives men their existence but leaves it to them to write their own history. The proof of this is precisely that at the end of human history God will recapitulate this history by fulfilling the will of man and giving him the perfect city.

The New Jerusalem ?

Exactly. God said to man more or less this : "In the beginning I gave you a garden to live in which was the Garden of Eden ; but in the end you did not want it. You preferred your own city which was raised up against me - the door was built there to keep God out - but at the end of Time - because your cities have always been unbearable places -, I shall give you a GOOD city which will correspond to what you have always desired."

So it isn't simply a metaphor, it's a real city ?

Chapter 11

Indeed it is. But it isn't as you would imagine with monuments and public squares, etc. We cannot know just yet what this ideal city will be like but what is very important is that it is certainly a city that we shall find at the end. Moreover this is one of the major differences between Judeo-Christian theology and the majority of religious myths which believe that in the end we go back to the same place : the Garden of Eden before the Fall.

The God of the Bible takes into consideration the will of man. It is not a city that will have been built in heaven and sent down to earth, ready to be lived in, but a city which condenses, which recapitulates the individual and collective history of man. "All the nations shall bring their works" say the Scriptures. The city, where the revolts against God occur, will become the place of reconciliation. By doing this God proves to man that he is at his side throughout his whole journey.

Will the New Jerusalem be on the site of the present Jerusalem ?

I have no idea. We are told that it will come down from heaven but we are not told where it will be set up. As in all prophesies what happens in the end has something to do with the prophesy but is not necessarily followed to the letter.

But if it is to be a very real city it will become one with the whole planet ?

Perhaps. It is also possible that it could extend beyond the limits of the planet. I simply cannot say. Traditionally there are some stupid questions asked about this of the kind : "How many billions of men will live in this city ? and how will God cope ?" These are questions which concern the almightiness of God, and it's not for me to try to answer them.

What is it that best defines the specificity of the God that you believe in ?

There is no better reply to that question than the words spoken by Jesus Christ when he told us that "God is Love.". The fullness of love.

According to you God does whatever he wishes but does not do or make every possible thing ?

Precisely. God does not cause everything to be or to happen. When I say that he does as he wishes, this means that he is free to "do or make" events happen or people exist. And "what he wishes" does not encompass each man and the whole of mankind.

Nevertheless this God does intervene in History ?

God does intervene at specific moments in History. You can witness this by referring to the Bible. In the Old Testament for example, the history of the kings illustrates well the fact that God did not dictate how they should behave. These kings - be it Saul or David - behaved as they felt inclined, sometimes in accordance with God's will and sometimes not.

On several occasions you have said that we are in a period when God is silent. When did this period of desertion begin ? Why is God silent ?

We always tend to take a truncated view of history. You shouldn't forget that biblically speaking God makes very rare interventions over periods lasting hundreds of years. In the same way God only speaks on rare occasions. Just think, the events recorded in the Bible go back to the year fourteen hundred before Christ, and what is there ? The Old Testament runs to seven or eight hundred pages, and within them there are in fact a very small number of times that we find the word of God.

And what is more, at the end of the Book of Kings, if I remember rightly, one can find the following statement : "This was a time when God was silent." This shows us clearly that at certain periods God did not speak, he simply let man get on by himself ; until such time as a prophet was called up. So we can spread our modest knowledge to those believers around us, in our small way we can bear witness to God's goodness while awaiting the appearance of a prophet among us.

We should be careful not to lable people as prophets too quickly, as some people have done for Barth and even for myself.*(Laughs)* We mustn't do that. My words would then take on a significance and force that they do not have, if I was conveying the Word of God.

What if I were to say to you that your conception of God is nothing more than an artifice to avoid tackling the really embarrassing questions ?

I would reply that you have a false idea of God.*(Laughs)* Whether it be the philosophers' conception, or that of the theorists who have ONE particular image of God. There you must be careful - we'll only ever have a certain image of God we'll never have anything else ! And to describe God as being incognito comes done to saying that at that particular moment God had refused the image we had made of him.

So it for that reason, in a certain sense, I agreed with the theology of the death of God. If this involves saying that God - in himself- is dead, which is idiotic, then this means nothing at all. But if we say that the image of God that was used in the nineteenth century no longer pertains, that image of God is dead, then I am in total agreement. The only thing we can kill is the image of God !

How do you propose to make the distinction between true and false prophets ?

There are many false prophets. The image that springs to mind concerning that is the painting - the crucifixion of Grünewald - where you can see at one side of the cross a group of women weeping and on the other side there is John the Baptist. John the Baptist is pointing at Jesus, what is very surprising is that he has a disproportionately long finger which many people have noted but no-one has explained. This is the picture of a true prophet, a prophet who is saying : "Look not at me but behold Him"

You end a letter that you published in the review the "Semeur" in January 1939 with this admission : "I do not enjoy playing the role of the perpetual protestor or little prophet tucked away in his corner." You already had these thoughts at that time ?

(Laughs) Within the Protestant community I was classified exactly like that. Even at that stage they saw that I had a protestant side - in the worst sense of the word : the perpetual protestor - on the other hand they were also beginning to refer to me as a "prophet", I refused to be considered as such.

That said, there is a permanent misunderstanding going on. By the word "prophet" people generally understand someone who foresees the future ; now this is not the correct definition of the biblical prophets.

Someone who brings the Word of God ?

Yes a prophet is someone who announces the Word of God at a particular moment during a historic event. During the historic event the prophet is there to witness the Word of God. In that respect the prophecies are different from the Gospels, which record the event after it has occurred.

Can you explain why people saw you as a prophet ?

They thought they saw the prophet in me because of my attempt to analyse the political events of the period 1937-1938. For example I was in disagreement with Suzanne de Dietrich who wrote articles in the *Semeur* concerning events in Czechoslovakia, she felt that we should have sent in the army as soon as Germany invaded the Sudetenland.

Ever since that period that reproach made about you by Suzanne de Dietrich was to become a recurrent theme : your tendency to consider that all cats at night are grey. You refused to come down in favour of imperfect democracies over outright dictatorships.

I never assimilated the two. All the same I did belong to every single antifascist movement I could find. Only what I wanted to fight against was that good conscience which enabled democracies to state : "We are right." I believed that we should indeed fight dictatorships but also always be mindful that our very own democracies contain their own dose of dictatorship.

Yes, but it is easy for us to say that you do not come down on any side when you refuse to see a difference between freedom in France to slavery in

Germany, on the pretext that they are in fact quite comparable. In the France of 1938 at least Christians could express themselves freely, couldn't they?

Yes they could express something that would be drowned in the flood of information and publications, and which had no importance whatsoever. In the same way as I entertain very few illusions concerning the importance of what I myself have written.

At that period you were to say of the Munich agreements: "They are not as important as all that." "Isn't that shocking when you think of the fate awaiting the Jews, the Spanish republicans and even the Czechs?

For me there was a world of difference between intellectual stand-points and actual involvement or commitment. For example we threw our support wholeheartedly behind the Spanish republicans. In the same way, how could I possibly have overlooked the Czech question when my aunt and all the paternal side of my family lived over there? I was not at all indifferent to what was happening and I intervened whenever I possibly could.

But I did not believe that this should be turned into an international question, to be decisive for the whole of Europe, which is the way it was presented at the time. There was absolutely no doubt in my mind that we had to destroy Hitler and Nazi doctrine. I was always completely uncompromising concerning fascist movements.

I don't doubt that, what I was alluding to was your constant refusal to choose the the camp of the Western democracies.

It is a fact that I am unable to say that on one side there is Good and the other Evil. I simply can't do that.

Yes but when absolute Evil puts something that is relatively good in jeopardy, it is surely the duty of a Christian to stand up for the side of Good?

Of course, I was able to demonstrate that in the Resistance, we must combat absolute Evil. When the point is reached that human-beings are despised to that extent, that is absolute Evil. But this doesn't entitle us to presume, with a clear conscience, that we represent Good for all that. This combat must be undertaken in the same way that a detective goes out to arrest a criminal, knowing full well that we will be forced to get our hands dirty by using means that are not good.

You never rallied to the defense of the pluralist model during the Cold War, is that because of your excessively idealistic view of democracy?

For me democracy can only function as a real democracy when it is truly direct, hence it can only function in very small units. That is why I have always been a federalist. It would be possible to have a democracy in each *département* in

Chapter 11

France, where each citizen would be able to vote directly on matters as they arose. I do not believe in representative democracy at all. Our Western regimes are not democracies in my eyes since the decisions are not made by the people.

But can democracy ever be anything other than people choosing people to lead them ?

The leaders are not chosen by the people for the reason that they already constitute a political CLASS, in other words it's always the same people who come back and who support each other.

So you would not defend this imperfect democracy ?

If I had to choose between several types of regime it is obvious that I would settle for an imperfect democracy over a dictatorship any time. There's no doubt about that. Simply what I am trying to dismantle is the ideology. I will not have anyone trying to convince me that it is the model of democracy. No, that is not what democracy is.

Is it Rousseau's model, then ?

Yes, if you like ; it is Rousseau's model or that of ancient Athens. In ancient Athens everything was decided at the "Boule" it was the assembly of citizens which decided on the laws that were presented to them.

That is all very well but Athenian democracy excluded women, slaves and metics, didn't it ?

That's true. It didn't involve the whole population.

CHAPTER TWELVE

Human nature. Natural law. Incarnation. God. Hell. A possible impossibility. Technology and authority. Pessimism. The man of faith and the man of science. The *exousiai*. God in History. An arbitrary god ? Microcomputing and revolution.

Patrick CHASTENET - *You insist on the importance of milieu and you refute the existence of human nature. So logically how can you reconcile this stance with a belief in one God at the source of all life ?*

Jacques ELLUL - Of course all human beings keep their specificity before God but I do not believe that there is a natural law governing human nature. It is true that the man who fulfils his task, however meagre his basic lot may have been, is the man who has forged his own existence. He has done so through his own society and his own institutions. What leads me to challenge this idea of human nature is the prodigious diversity of customs and institutions. If there was really only one sort of human nature than all these customs and institutions should be the same. As it turns out one finds institutions that are entirely specific to one given social entity compared with the others.

You have mentioned natural law. However even if you insist on the diversity that exists surely there are some constants that appear ?

I do not believe at all in the existence of universal values. For us, in our society, human life is sacred. But, just think, there are some societies where it is only when a boy has killed a man that he is accepted as an adult, killing is the sign of manhood. In our society it is entirely different. And what is meant by the rights of children for example ? They have no meaning whatsoever if there is no way of exercising them. As far as I am concerned Law is inseparable from the possibility of it being exercised. With natural law we are up to our necks in ideology.

You consider that the theme of incarnation is essential. For you Jesus is God ?

What is really fundamental is the way we conceive of God. Either he is transcendent, and only transcendent, far removed from men and thus remains the sovereign Judge. This idea of God is the traditional one. Now what Jesus Christ taught us was that God came down to man and this is very important because traditionally man always tried to go up towards God. Man did this through mysticism or as the giants did piling up mountains on top of one after another in their attempts to reach up to God.

What we learn from the Bible, particularly through the teachings of Jesus, is that God is not inaccessible as we had once thought, but that he has come down to earth to man's level and that he is not just a God of judgement. He is of course a God of Judgement, but he is also the God who so loves man that he suffers all that man does. "I stretched out to you and implored you", says the Old Testament. God implores us and stretches out to us. When God speaks to man and asks : "My people, what is it that I have done that you treat me so ?", he is the God of love as Jesus has told us he would be.

From this I draw the conclusion that Hell does not exist. For me all men are saved as Saint Paul tells us : "According to whether you built in gold, marble, wood or straw your work will be destroyed or survive at the Day of Judgement. But you yourself will be saved." In other words nothing of my life may survive, everything will be wiped out, as if consumed by fire, but I will be redeemed in God.

So, like Barth, you think that Hell remains a "possible impossibility" ?

(Laughs) It is clear that since God is free to do what he wants he could always make Hell exist. I cannot judge before the event. But I do find this hard to imagine of a God of Love. He shows his love, above all in Jesus Christ, which makes Hell impossible. Because he is God Almighty he can create whatever he wishes, and so he can create Hell. As Barth said : "You have to be crazy to teach universal salvation but you are impious of you do not believe in it."

You insist that God is Love, but you demonstrate that he is both Love and Justice. If we insist on the Justice aspect surely Hell reappears as a possibility ?

God's justice is revealed to us through Jesus Christ. Everything was fulfilled through Jesus. There is no other justice of God than that which condemned Jesus Christ in the name of all men. And after the crucifixion we are all redeemed in that very love. Biblical thinking is dialectic. It is enough to go through the Old Testament to realize that after the passages of condemnation and intimidation always come words of promise and blessing !

Does that mean to say that, after all, we are already living this hell on earth ?

Man already has more than his share of woes on this earth and God would not add to that. On the contrary he came down to earth to console his children. I believe that men between themselves create their own hell. Let's face it we have had some rather flagrant examples of this in recent times.

Is it being optimistic or pessimistic to think that we are already experiencing hell here on earth ?

Chapter 12

I am by nature rather pessimistic. My first view of things is always bleak, I see what doesn't work or what may turn out not to work. On the other hand my faith in Jesus Christ necessarily makes me optimistic. That was what has made it possible for me take on my work with young delinquents, in the hope of improving their lot.

Does the belief that hell is here on earth not incite you to take an even darker view in your analysis of social issues ?

(Laughs) That accusation is often levelled against me. Quite honestly however I believe that my theological convictions and stance in no way interfere with the way I study society. I do everything within my power to keep the influence of my faith separate from both my sociological analysis and my work as a historian. My quest has always been for exactitude and not for *the truth*. I really don't think that I have overlooked any aspects of reality. I was only too happy when I came across something positive in the world and when I perceived a positive human outcome. But that only happened on rare occasions.

On the one hand you point out that Jesus spurned power and chose the path of meakness and on the other you say that technology is the instrument of power. Your sociology is not, according to you, conditioned by your reading of the Bible. How do you explain, therefore, that the exousiai *of the New Testament pop up in your scientific papers ?*

Technology is already a form of power to the extent that it enables man to achieve by force what he would otherwise have been unable to do. Indeed Technology does seem to me to be a *force* to be contended with in this world. This brings us only one step away from theology.

From a theological point of view force is something that is not just material and concrete but which is also spiritual. The *exousiai* are the forces ruled by God but which in reality are extremely restricting. In the Bible the *exousiai* appear as money and political power. It is not unreasonable to say that Technology is the *exousia* of the present day, with the spiritual force that that represents.

Do these exousiai *correspond to Jaspers' "anonymous forces" ?*

The *exousiai* are rather like the angels in the Creation and partially belong to the heavenly sphere. They are ruled and judged by God alone. When Christ was crucified it says quite clearly in the Scriptures that it was the *exousiai* - the earthly forces- that had crucified him. Jesus had deliberately chosen not to outdo these *exousiai* by using his might, thereby remaining entirely respectful of his Father. The example that he set was exactly that we must turn down that force, this meant that he would be delivered to the *exousiai* and he would go through to the complete sacrifice by being divested of everything.

This was his choice, he could have done otherwise, he said so himself when they came to arrest him and Peter wanted to defend him Jesus said to him : "Put up your sword. If I wanted to I could call up twelve legions of angels to my side. If I wanted to.. but I don't. I must be arrested, judged, put to death ; all this I must accept. For it is God's will."

These forces have rather an ambivalent status : they remain under God's command. So we can hardly write them off as forces of evil, can we ?

Anyway God would not be God if there were a force against him to counterbalance him. We can see from the Bible that the forces of evil are always very limited in efficiency. Satan is *Shatan*, the accuser, and that is the extent of his role. The Devil, the *diabolos*, is the one who creates divisions. Therefore it is not possible to attribute any universality to these forces of evil. For the *exousias* it's the same thing each one has its own specific role to play.

An exousia *cannot be reduced to a* diabolos. *By saying that politics, the State or technology are* exousiai, *isn't this tantamount to saying....*

It is not tantamount to saying that they are Satan or the Devil.

But they can be one or the other ?

They can let themselves be possessed.

This is not by their nature, but brought about by the circumstances ?

It is precisely brought on by the circumstances.

So they can go either way ?

Yes, yes.

And are they still under God's command ?

Obviously, they remain under God's command. God has such respect for what he has created and for his creatures that he respects their laws, even if this idea is hard to accept. If you look for examples of God intervening directly in the Old Testament, you will find that in a period of over one thousand two hundred years he only does so on four or five occasions. That is very few times. When you consider the miracles wrought by Jesus, the miraculous healing he brought about, if God had so wanted there could have been no more illness of course. But illness is part of the natural order and the nature of man. This is very important for me, God is not the *Deus ex Machina*, he is not there to make the machine work. He set the machine in motion, from then on he respects its liberty from him. That shows how much he is the God of Love !

What would you give as illustrations of God's intervention in History ?

Chapter 12

It is very difficult indeed to be sure that one is in the presence of divine intervention. Take Joan of Arc as an example. I can easily concede that she was inspired by God, but what she did was her responsibility and hers alone. Exactly the same thing with all the saints, whatever they actually did was their own responsibilty, God wasn't driving them like horses. God inspires you, God gets you started in life then it's up to you how you live your life.

Is that why you say that God is arbitrary just as love is arbitrary ?

What I wanted to say was that you cannot rationalize love, you can't bend it to your will, no more than you can forbid it. Either you love or you don't love. That is the way it is for me at least. And I would say that it is the same for God. When God says : "I have chosen Jacob and I have turned Esau away", that is perfectly arbitrary. Particularly when we usually misinterpret this and believe that God actually condemned Esau. What it really means is that it wasn't Esau but Jacob that God had chosen to convey the word of God. Esau was to live his life peacefully, and if God had not chosen him to carry out a particular mission he certainly didn't punish or condemn him for all that. Just like Cain, he remained under God's protection. From a theological point of view this is very important.

God chooses as he pleases. His choice is as arbitrary as the love that exists between this or that man and this or that woman. God does not make his choices according to any human criteria. Morally speaking, Jacob is to be condemned from every point of view. He was a liar, he was dishonest, he had cheated his brother of his birth-right, and in spite of all this he was the one that God chose. God is free. God is sovereign. But above all he is, in the words of Kierkegaard, the *Inconditionné* - with no conditions.

So God is arbitrary but not unjust ?

He would be unjust if he were to condemn his creatures to Hell. But as I have already said, Hell does not exist. When God says : "I turned Esau away", this is in a historical sense. Esau would no longer be the one from whom the chosen people would spring. That does not mean that he was damned.

That would be contrary to a God of love for everyone ?

There is love for everyone. Simply there are those whom God selects who can serve in the scheme of life and others whom God has left to live their lives and that is all. They are not useful to God's plan.

Does this mean that he loves some less than others ?

No, it's not like that he doesn't love some less but he does use some and not use others.

Jacques Ellul

In La Raison d'être *you wonder if God will remember any of the many thousands of pages you have covered with ink.*

Maybe God will remember just one. That would be wonderful. That is what the Apocalypse tells us - where in the perfect city - God will reconsider and synthesize the whole of man's history.

In 1937, in substance you wrote that it was still far too soon to say but technology could become a liberating factor for man. By 1972 [1], you felt it was too late, but in 1981 [2] you claimed that it was still possible to take technology in hand. This note of hope disappeared entirely in Le Bluff technologique [3]

With a new global technology like computer science, man could quite well have mastered the technological system and changed its orientation. In the end I realized that instead of using information technology to liberate man from the shackles of technology, man had reintegrated it in the system and enhanced its power. In others words there had been an opening to establish the roles offered by this new technology but man chose to overlook it.

What do you expect of microcomputering ?

It seems to me that microinformatics could enable man to bring technological power down to its just level. But instead of freeing himself from the shackles of this technology he has surrendered to further intrusion into his personal life. Because of lack of imagination and will-power, man has become subordinate to informatics instead of being its master.

Does your analysis apply only to France ?

No. Only it is easier for me to work on the French case. But France is highly representative - unlike the United States - precisely because there is nothing in her past to prepare her for such an influence for such a mutation. This also implies that the force of this technology is very considerable to have been able to go against, what was until the nineteen hundreds, the course of French history.

A more general question now. Which of the books you have written do you prefer ?

I would say that it is the book that I wrote on hope [4]. I put my whole heart into writing that book.

And in sociology ?

It has to be *La Technique*.

Chapter 12

[1] *De la Révolution aux révoltes.* (From the revolution to the revolt)
[2] *Changer de Révolution* was written in 1981. (Change revolutions.)
[3] Published in 1988.
[4] *L'Espérance oubliée.* (Hope forgotten)

CHAPTER THIRTEEN

Technology. Technological society and ecological thinking. Man and nature. Progress. Consciousness raising. A misunderstanding. Political party or counter force ? A more frugal society. The economic programme of the Greens. Genesis.

Patrick CHASTENET - *How would you summarize the main thrust of your work on technology ?*

Jacques ELLUL - I would say that I have tried to show how technology is developing completely independently of any human control. Carried away in some Promethean dream modern man has always thought he could harness Nature whereas what is happening is that he is building an artificial universe for himself where he is increasingly being constrained. He thought he would achieve his goal by using technology but he has ended up its slave. The means have become the goals and necessity a virtue.

We have become conditioned in such a way that we take on every new technology without once wondering about its possible harmfulness. There is nothing worrying about technology as such but our attitude towards it is very worrying.

What links are there between your criticism of technological society and ecological thinking ?

They are very close that is for sure. I think the ecologists have the right and sensible attitude towards the environment but as far as doctrine is concerned I find them rather narrow and naive. They tend to polarize their efforts on limited objectives without taking into account all the consequences of technology on the human psyche. There is a modification taking place in our being that the ecologists don't envisage.

What is more technology is not the only cause of destruction of Nature. Technology may accelerate changes however we should never lose sight of the fact that what we call Nature today is in fact the product of hundreds of years of man's interaction with the environment. For example when you take a walk through the forest in the Landes you have the impression that this is Nature in its pure state, well it isn't. Its an artifcial forest planted by man.

Do you consider the ecologists as your spiritual heirs.

It is true to say that the work that Bernard Charbonneau and I did laid the foundation stones of a certain ecological thought. However I do believe that what ecologists lack is an overall grasp of technical phenomena and the technological society. It is all very well to attack the factories at Seveso but it's necessary to assume the consequences this will have on the rest of industrial production.

They don't seem to understand that the technological system is just that, it is a "system", so it it pointless to attack an isolated element. One must tackle the problem as a whole. One can't really hope to protect Nature without putting the very structures of our society into question.

Ecologists are often criticized for being against progress, and you yourself are even described as being a technophobe. What is your answer to the allegation that both these attitudes are in the strict sense of the word "retrograde".

(Laughs) It amuses me to answer that kind of comment by pointing out that it is the backward thrust of a jet engine which enables us to travel forward so fast. I'm the same kind of backward force. But I have no wish whatsoever to return to the past. Even since Taylor invented his time and motion model people have been insisting that man must adapt to technology but surely it should be the other way round.

All we have to do is rebuild a society where the ordinary man is no longer completely subordinated to technology in his work or in his leisure. This is a difficult objective to achieve because we are dominated by phenomena which go beyond us and which leave us no time to choose.

We could do without 90% of the technological equipment we use and 90% of the drugs that we take, but the force of the propaganda machine is such that it transforms useless objects into necessities. Our needs have been artificially established by advertizing and now they continue naturally.

Bernard Charbonneau and you have always claimed that the first thing to do is to make people aware of problems. At the recent elections the ecologists scored 15% of the votes and enjoy an even bigger popular sympathy, would you say that political ecology is proving its worth ?

I'm not at all sure about that. I think that the present balance of powers rests on a misunderstanding. Did people vote in favour of ecology or against the traditional political parties ? As far as I'm concerned I've always stayed faithful to anarcho-syndicalism as it was in the early days of the movement. Ecology has nothing to gain from being transformed into a political party or running an electoral campaign. According to me ecology should develop as a counter force but should never indulge in politicking.

I dream of a balanced society in which any ideologically motivated group would, by virtue of its numbers of followers, be able to stand up to and correct the state power. It is certainly not through the political system that we are going to be able to change the orientation taken by our industry or reduce the hold that technology has on our society.

Politics can solve none of our fundamental problems. If we really want to come to grips with these problems we will have to make a complete change in our

Chapter 13

life style. We'll have to give up all the things that make our lives easier, and let's not fool ourselves we will have to go back to frugal ways. It is not at all sure that everyone who voted for the ecologists would be prepared to make all those sacrifices.

But you do go along with the Greens' economic policies i.e. stopping the nuclear program, closing down all nuclear facilities within ten years, rethinking the car, development of public transport, challenging productionism, radically reducing working hours (with a thirty hour week by the beginning of the twenty first century) and job-sharing to bring down unemployment figures.

I'm all the more in favour of the main issues on this program as you may remember Bernard Charbonneau and I were already advocating wide-spread reduction of working hours and job-sharing back in the thirties. This is perfectly possible and absolutely indispensible. Sharing out the work to be done will probably involve increased production costs but this will be off-set by reductions in compensation allowances and the costs of un-employment.

Competition from abroad is used as an argument against this type of proposal. But surely one could argue that if France were to adopt such projects this could serve as an example and that other countries would follow suit. No-one can deny that this is a global problem. How long must we go on thinking in terms of production alone ? The reasoning of those who govern us is fifty years out of date. It never even occurs to them that we could orientate our economy towards activities that are useful but not necessarily productive.

To counter his solitude man needs genuine human relationships, recreational activities and personal contact other than those he makes at the work-place. We must break out of this vicious circle of consuming and producing, even if this means undoing our daily habits and reducing our standards of living.

What is the Christian stance on ecology ? How must we understand the command in Genesis to "subdue Nature" ?

In fact that's a mistranslation. This was a command that man received before the fall, before he broke with God. Moreover just before this injunction is mentioned it says that God had created man in his own image. So it should read : "Rule, make order, and subdue nature as God has done, in other words with loving care". Man's job is to preserve and cultivate this world and not to drain and impoverish it. The North American Indians when they used to hunt bison would always take care to leave enough bison to ensure that there would be future generations. Whereas today we seem to have forgotten this rudimentary law, that it is simply not possible to carry on developing endlessly in a finite universe.

CHAPTER FOURTEEN

Human stud farms. Genetic engineering. Man the guinea-pig. Ambivalence of technological progress. The State and bio-ethics. Voluntary Termination of Pregnancy. The Church and morality. The State faced with miracles. Organ donors. The Bible and blood. The body and eternal life. Gene therapy. Biology and the race struggle. The Church and cloning. Medically assisted pregnancies. *Biological adultery.*

PATRICK CHASTENET - *As early as 1948 you were talking about "human stud farms" wouldn't you say that the fact that the scientific community is now taking the ethical aspect of their research very seriously rather contradicts your argument concerning the automatism of technological progress ?*

JACQUES ELLUL.- It is true at least as far as genetic engineering is concerned, that the scientists have decided to call a halt to certain practices. This doesn't mean that all research in this field has been stopped. What I'm afraid of is that one scientist will decide to go just one step further and that will turn out to be one step too far.

You believe that according to technological logic if it is possible to do something then it should be done ?

Yes. Everything that is technically possible ends up being carried out. You get used to this. Initially people are shocked at what seems abominable or scandalous and then little by little they get used to it.

Do you still believe that we are being used as "human guinea-pigs", I'm thinking particularly of the experiments carried out on pregnant women in the United States ?

This is still a very topical issue. Nowadays certain drugs whose side effects are unknown are tested on human beings. This is all done for the benefit of mankind of course.
I was struck by the instructions in the drugs I'm taking at the moment which always list the undesirable side-effects. In order to overcome these side-effects I'm given yet more drugs which have their own undesirable side-effects and so it goes on.

Jacques Ellul

So that is a good illustration of the ambivalence of technological progress ?

Exactly. Technology provides use with cures for our ills by creating further ills. They know very well that the intravenous transfusions that they give me throw my system right out of sync. They are curing me, or at least they are preventing my lymphoma from spreading, at the same time they are unbalancing the rest of me.

Do you think it is the role of the State to legislate such matters as medically assisted pregnancies, in vitro fertilization, and bio-ethics in general ?

I don't think so. If a man's life is not in danger why should the State intervene ? The State is not the guardian of morality. In fact that is a problem that can be addressed by the counter forces within society. What the Church, backed by its members, has to say on the matter should be a deciding factor. But the Church has become so discredited because of political stances it has taken or compromises of all kinds that we can no longer have complete confidence in it.

When I was on the board of Bagatelle Hospital we set up the first centre in Bordeaux for the termination of pregnancies, but naturally we took all possible precautions. Any woman wanting a termination had to consult not only a doctor but also a psychologist and she had to give her reasons. Every path was explored to be sure that termination was the only way out of the woman's dilemma.

So you claim that the Church and not the State is the guarantor of morality. But what about atheists, there are quite a lot of them you know ?

If the Church was doing its job properly, if it took the courageous stances that it should take, I am convinced that non-believers would have confidence in the Church's position. The Church has totally fallen in everyone's esteem and it has brought down esteem for the Christian faith with it.
If there are so many non-believers today it is because we Christians have not been up to the job we had to do.

In the Christ de Montfavet [1] scandal in 1954, you condemned the sect of the visionary post office worker but you denied that the State had the right to force parents, who believe that faith alone can heal, to use official medical treatment, didn't you ?

Indeed, the State puts up with institutionalized miracles, take Lourdes for example, but the State will not tolerate anyone wishing to live according to their own vision of the truth. The modern State is not anti-Christian but rather against any incarnation of faith.
The only miracle healings that can occur are those brought about in the name of Jesus Christ. I am too respectful of the honour of God to mix him up in everything we do. In fact the miracles that Jesus performed were all miracles of love and not of power. What bothers me with the majority of miracles that are announced

Chapter 14

today is precisely that they are announced. It is in this way that the proclamation of the miracle becomes a sort of instrument of power, of publicity. But how many times did Jesus say : "You are whole go your way in peace." In other words "don't advertize what has happened." ?

Have you ever witnessed a miracle ?

There is at least one that I witnessed which will probably amuse you and that I can tell you about. There was a family that lived in a haunted house. It was a truly amazing haunted house, I saw it with my own eyes. Pieces of furniture moved around by themselves, there was knocking on the walls and sounds coming out of the ceiling etc. To cut a long story short the family was at its wit's end. So one day the local minister asked if I would mind going and performing an exorcism. I had nothing against trying, so we devised a sort of liturgy for the exorcism which worked very well as it turned out.

But Protestants don't practise exorcism, do they ?

We Protestants are very rational so normally that is not the sort of thing we would go in for. But in this particular case I have to admit it worked.

You dismiss both the progressives and the traditionalists over the question of bio-ethics in the name of the integrity of man and true love. But what happens to a couple who love each other but cannot conceive by "normal" means, must they bow to their fate ?

No, not at all. This is the contrary of termination of pregnancy. It seems perfectly legitimate to me to use any scientific method available to conceive a child. I can see nothing wrong with that.

I wanted to get that quite clear because one does get the impression from what you have written that one must not let science intervene in the course of Nature to preserve man's integrity.

In this case there is no interference in the process of Nature precisely because there is no process. So here it is man who sets the process in action. The natural mechanisms all exist as such and it is not at all God who makes the machine work.

Yes but you know very well that there are some Christians for whom the fact that they cannot conceive is God's will ?

That corresponds to the point of view that God influences our lives at all times. Now God loves us, more than anything, he gave his son to die for us but he certainly does not direct every step we take, on the contrary. What God wants most for us is liberty. After we have used this liberty that he has given us he will judge how we have fared.

God initiated the creation but after that creation has continued to evolve according to its own laws.

To get back to genetic engineering. You say that the implication underlying this technique is the negation of man as a human-being. In other words that man is a robot, is nothing more than a collection of spare parts. Within this logical framework are you hostile to the donation of organs ?

I'm very uncomfortable about this because I believe, without going so far as to say that we are overstepping the limits of what life allows, that organ transplants are part and parcel of technology's creation. To give you an example which will make my position perfectly clear, I have always said that I would refuse to receive a blood transfusion. Moreover the Bible tells us in no uncertain terms that it is forbidden to mix blood.

But aren't you making a too literal interpretation there ?

You must always begin by making a literal interpretation of the Bible otherwise you could miss out all kinds of things. Once you refuse to take the Bible literally you can use historical or interpretive reasons for discarding passages that don't suit you. So you must first accept the passage for what it is and then proceed to a theological, interpretive or historical examination of its content. But the first impact must be what the passage says to you.

What is the explanation given in the Bible for forbidding the mixing of blood ?

The Bible tells us our blood is our soul therefore it is what constitutes our being. Now you cannot mix beings. Each being must retain its own integrity.

Indeed but when we know that organ transplants can save lives and help people to live better ?

I'm not systematically opposed to organ transplants but I would like people to realize that life is not the end of everything. For me, life on Earth is not the ultimate. So we die, we die. I was going to say that there is nothing dramatic about that. What is dramatic is the separation that occurs. That is dramatic, but not death itself.

Has the fact that you are against blood transfusions and organ transplants anything to do with keeping our bodies intact for the Day of Judgement ?

Yes. It is obvious that our bodies are very important even for our eternal life. Saint Paul is quite clear on this subject. Our bodies are born corruptible but will

Chapter 14

rise incorruptible, are born weak but will rise strong, are born contemptible but will rise in glory. So never think for one moment that you can mix up bodies. (Laughs)

So giving your body to science is not an innocent operation?

It is most certainly not an innocent operation but I believe that God, in his goodness, will make allowances when the motives are sufficiently praiseworthy.

What are your views on genetic therapies which make it possible to avoid the transmission of hereditary defects by selecting unaffected embryos?

That doesn't strike me as any worse than the average surgical operation. To ensure that the child will be born healthy and without the threat of disease is entirely beneficial.

Yes of course. But what do you think of the "slippery slope" towards the evil embrace of eugenics that the opponents of genetic therapy so apprehend?

My position has always been the same. When we know how to do something then we do it. We always have the possiblity to control the use of the technique as we did for the terminations that I mentioned before. But I don't hold out great illusions. It is obvious that once we have these techniques very soon we'll push them to the limits.

Some people advocate the use foetal screening but only in a therapeutic context and never for personal convenience. Other people reject this distinction, for them biology has reached the heights of Western reason. They would even favour using this technological progress to improve the genetic structure of man. What do you think?

I am closer to the second group. Anyway I think that it is inevitable considering the state of our technological development. It would require a spiritual philosophy which transcends all others and which is accepted by everyone for this kind of development to be stopped. What is sure is that it won't be stopped by good morality or reasonable arguments.

Do you believe that Western scientists are trying to make a "superior" race or at least an improved one?

Obviously Western technology wants to make man superior. The question is to know what is meant by superior. Because if it is taken to mean stronger, or if it is taken to mean adaptation to the technological world then I don't think that superior is the right word.

If however the goal is to make a man who is kinder, more open to others, honest, loving and charitable, which I highly doubt, then I can see no harm in going ahead, but if it is to be imposed from the outside I say no. Man's moral make-up comes from a series of decisions that he makes for himself, but in the case in hand these decisions would be taken for him, they would even be taken in advance. One cannot play at being God.

According to the grid that you usually apply to such things the experiments on cloning human cells that were carried out in 1993 are liable to be generalized in the future?

Exactly. It's always the same problem. You cannot stop things happening from the outside. There is no reason that the State should get mixed up in this. There will always be endless debates between the political parties on the one side and the scientific community on the other, which will in turn be split between those who foresee the dangers ahead and those who want to forge ahead to see how far they can push back the frontiers.

If you don't think it falls to the politicians to conduct these debates, who do you think should?

If only the Churches had authority and if they kept abreast of the situation of man in the modern world then it is obvious it would be their role. But the awful thing is that the Churches always tackle these problems with a mealy-mouthed piety and take a moralistic stance.

There are certain scientists today who are manifesting their concern about these matters, is this a sign of growing awareness?

It is very interesting to observe that the scientists who are sounding the alarm are not less considered for taking a moral stance. People are beginning to listen to them, even in the media. It is not impossible that the great turn-about in attitudes will come from the scientists themselves.

One often finds that doctors are the most reluctant to perform certain treatments on ethical grounds...

Exactly. In the world of technology there is nothing to stop cloning being used more and more extensively but I think that may give rise to waves of revulsion in certain sectors of the population. It is my belief that modern man has no wish whatsoever to live in Huxley's Brave New World.

Would you say that Nature shows us the limits we should not exceed. Take for example the menopause as a sign that it was too late to try artificial reproduction?

I think that's right. There are a certain number of facts about life that one must accept. One should listen to what Nature tries to tell us. At the menopause a woman who has already had a child must accept that her role in that domain is over.

Chapter 14

These are all problems to be solved using wisdom and spirituality, which are the most difficult things for modern man to turn to.

You have used the expression "biological adultery" to denounce sperm banks, isn't that rather over-evaluating biological filiation ? What does parenting mean to you, reproduction or up-bringing ?

Reproduction and up-bringing are part of one and the same thing. The biological component is very important. It is wonderful to recognize certain of one's own features in one's children or grand-children.

As far as I am concerned I would never have been able to accept a child conceived by donor as a child of my own. Such children would always be the children of some unknown person who had contributed a few drops of sperm. I have the impression that I would have been unable to give all my love to children conceived in such a way. Adoption seems a much healthier solution.

---

[1] Georges-Ernest Roux (1903-1981), a faith-healer who claimed to be Christ, founded a sect, which exists still today, in which using medecin is forbidden. The deaths of several followers from lack of conventional treatment triggered the scandal.

CHAPTER FIFTEEN

Bach and Mozart. Léo Ferré. The Threepenny Opera. Delacroix. Michelangelo. Villon. Hugo. Péguy. The empire of nonsense(Art in the technological Society). Dali. Structuralism. Klee. *Guernica*. Art split asunder. Chilling perfection. Art and technology.

Patrick CHASTENET - *You have made an analysis of the meaning of art in a technological society, but what are your personal tastes in music for example ?*

Jacques ELLUL - You must bear in mind that when I was young music didn't exist as it does today when young people are bathed in an atmosphere of music all the time. In those days we didn't have a gramophone, records or television. I didn't really hear any music before the age of twenty.

I remember once my friend Pouyanne took me along to a concert I couldn't make anything of the music. For me it was nothing but noise. Since I wasn't captivated by this noise I occupied myself making a sociological study of the people in the audience instead. It was only gradually that I came to like music. My wife played an important part in this. So I would say I'm a bit of a Philistine in the music department.

Of course I do have my favourite music which you may find rather commonplace. I like Bach and I like Mozart, nothing unusual I admit, but I do find something that appeals to me in their music. I feel comfortable listening to them. This is certainly not the case for ultramodern music be it high-brow or rock. I have been known to find the odd jazz musician such as Louis Armstrong most enjoyable, that is the exception rather than the rule. I dislike Romantic music.

Nowadays, since I lost my wife, I rarely listen to music. I would much sooner read or even read aloud, especially poetry, than even think of putting on a record.

Despite all that do you have a favourite musician ?

(Laughs) First of all I must confess to despising all kinds of opera even Mozart. I find opera so artificial in every respect. It is so untrue to life. We never express our feelings in the manner portrayed in opera. I can't find any relationship between the words and the music and even if it does exist it doesn't interest me.

On the other hand I am a fan of some contemporary singers such as Leo Ferré. But that is precisely because there is a real relation between the anarchist message he wanted to convey, which appealed to me, and the quality of his singing. The music and the words really went together.

As far as opera is concerned I'm prepared to make one exception. I always loved Kurt Weill's music and the songs in German in The Threepenny Opera.

Now for painting. What are your tastes there ?

I absolutely loathe eighteenth century painting. I much prefer fifteenth and sixteenth century works. In my view this was the great era of art with such artists as Michelangelo and Leonardo da Vinci. Among the Romantic painters, I am very fond of Delacroix, in particular one of his paintings which I go to see frequently here in the museum in Bordeaux : *La Grèce expirante sur les ruines de Missolonghi* (Greece breathing her last amid the ruins of Missolonghi)

Do you like sculpture ?

Yes, very much indeed. But I'm dreadfully classical in my tastes, because I like sculpture that represents something that is comprehensible. I have no time for sculptures which are nothing more than a bundle of shapes. Obviously the greatest sculptor for me is Michelangelo.

Generally speaking would you say you prefer figurative to conceptual art ?

Yes that's true. Moreover I don't understand why conceptual art is called conceptual, I see no concepts in it. In fact what is called non-figurative art is really the figurative art of the technological society.

Who are your favourite poets ?

I'll start with Villon, who is perhaps not exactly my favourite poet but he comes very close. In the sixteenth century there was after all Agrippa d'Aubigné, I like some of his work enormously, but he did write too much. He would have been well-advised to publish only a quarter of what he wrote. Even though Aubigné is more or less forgotten today, he is clearly familiar to the world of poetry because Victor Hugo lifted whole passages from him for his own use.

I can quote an example if you like. Aubigné writes of the resurrection as follows :
Et comme un bon nageur qui termine son plonge
Ils sortent de la mort comme l'on sort d'un songe [1]
these very lines turn up, word for word, in the writings of Victor Hugo.

Which is your favourite Villon ?

Every poem Villon wrote is my favourite. I can read and reread him and always feel the same pleasure. Any of his work be it the long or the short *Testament* or any of his *Ballades*. I appreciate his wit, especially just at the very moment he expected to be hanged he is able to write :
Et bientôt mon col

Chapter 15

saura que mon cul poise,

in other words : "my neck is soon to discover how much my ass weighs."

Who are your favourite more recent poets ?

I don't particularly care for the seventeenth and eighteenth century poets, but there again that is not my favourite period. As far as the Romantics are concerned my absolute preference is for Vigny, I'm sometimes moved by Victor Hugo's grandeur or Musset's charm. All that is very ordinary but there you are. Very often I recite Victor Hugo to myself because I find the sound of his poems beautiful. There is something very fine about *Le soir de bataille* :

Mon père ce héros au sourire si doux
Suivi d'un seul housard qu'il aimait entre tous
Pour sa grande bravoure et pour sa haute taille
Parcourait à cheval le soir d'une bataille
Le champ couvert de morts sur qui tombait la nuit. [2]

It's an old habit of mine to read poetry aloud for the pleasure of it. Let's get on with the list. I don't really like Rimbaud I prefer Baudelaire to him. But more than either of them I like such authors as Péguy and Saint-Jean Perse and then the modern poets René Char, Henri Michaux, Yves Bonnefoy or even Marie Noël.

You have written that the Rolling Stones don't make music they make one infernal racket. It strikes me that you are trying to justify the fact that you don't understand them when you write like that ?

Of course that's correct. I completely agree with you. I understand perfectly well that it may be possible to find something appealing in that noise if not exactly to like it. But it does nothing for me.

Is it possible to not like Stockhausen or Xenakis and still admit that it is music ?

For me it's all noise. I can feel no harmony I can find no meaning in it. All I see is that we have a tendency nowadays towards mindlessness where we let so many things numb our brains. I find it intolerable to wish to add this kind of noise on top of all that.

I know that you do not patronize the Centre for contemporary Plastic art in Bordeaux, do you feel the same about Beaubourg ?

No. I often visited the Beaubourg Centre when I was younger. I went because it interested me and out of curiosity. It was the ideal opportunity for me to research my book on contemporary art and the technological society.

Can you explain the meaning of Dali's statement that you quoted in L'Empire du non-sens *: "Paint, don't worry about being modern. That is the one* thing, unfortunately, that you won't be able to avoid being, no matter what ever else you do."

(Laughs) Dali had very well understood that whether we like it or not we are influenced by the period we live in. We can't behave as if the painting of the late nineteenth or early twentieth centuries never existed. We live in the period after they were painted and we have to get to know them not only so that we can distance ourselves from them but also quite simply because they exist. By knowing them we can't help being modern. My admiration for Dali knows no bounds.

Under these conditions what is modernity ?

Modernity is never something theoretical. It is a whole set of general ideas, prejudices, stereotypical judgements provided by society which we adopt without even realizing that we are doing so. In this sense painters are necessarily "modern" since they cannot escape being influenced by the current climate.

Is your Empire du non-sens *something more than just a simple illustration of your analyses of technology ?*

Indeed I would never claim that this book was a manifesto, but as I happened to grow up in an artistic environment because of my mother and that art has had an important place in my life, *L'Empire du non-sens* was also an expression, but not at all a judgement, of the influence of technology on art but directly on what modern art has brought me or not brought me.

Whatever happened to your project to write a book on Dubuffet ?

I have taken down loads of notes but I have never got round to writing them up. I admired Dubuffet enormously. I had wanted to explain how his painting expressed the modern world and illustrated a certain number of themes dear to me. With all the notes I have there's enough to keep me busy writing for at least ten years if ever I feel courageous enough to write some more books.

Can you explain why you feel technology kills meaning ?

To answer that I'd like to tell you a little anecdote. I once knew a theologian who was making a structuralist study of Biblical texts. Her work was always very serious and meticulous. When I asked her if structuralism helped her understand the meaning of the passage any better, she turned to me completely flabbergasted and said : "But there is no meaning." In other words what was important was how the text was structured, when I understand how the text is structured I understand all there is to know ! As far as I'm concerned such reasoning applied to a passage from the Bible is quite staggering.
If the structuralists are the servers of the text, in exactly the way I described forty years ago for the period of historical criticism, if one is trying to get to grips

Chapter 15

with a text and if one applies certain techniques in order to reach a better understanding then I see no harm in that. But if you simply apply techniques for the sake of applying techniques what is the point ?

I myself use the historico-criticism method and I can tell you that in Roman law we apply it even more seriously than the theologians have ever applied it to the Bible.

So for you structuralism is simply a technique ?

It is an instrument. And I am quite happy for it to be used as an instrument, but on the condition that it doesn't boil down to simply putting arrows all over the place to refer one word back to another. When one reads Claude Lévi-Strauss one realizes just how much structuralism is an instrument that he used to reach a better understanding of the subject he was studying. In his case the means were not confused with the ends.

Would you comment on the following quotation from Klee : "The more the world becomes a dreadful place the more horrible and abstract art becomes, and when the world is a happier place art seems to be more realistic" ?

That is always true. When the world is horrible you have the choice of representing it as more horrible still, or of doing abstract work where all that underlies the work is horrible. In Guernica Picasso expresses the tragedy that is taking place without showing piles of bloody flesh. The important thing in art is after all to transpose reality into an image which is sufficiently enthralling and meaningful so that the viewer gets an even better grasp of that reality.

Isn't the purpose of art also to help us escape from reality ?

I have never liked any form of escapism. I have always wanted to face reality whatever it may be. I have never wanted poetry to take me out of the world I live in but for it to give me a reason for living despite all adversity. Poetry is not a means of escape but a breath of fresh air in a world that is suffocating us. In the midst of all the actrocities one reads about in the papers, and one should know about them, it is absolutely life-saving for me to be able to read Péguy.

You describe "anti-establishment artists" as being Don Quichotte-like, as always behind the times, could you explain what you mean by that ?

Those that I've met at least, are always protesting against something that was true in the past whereas they themselves are in phase with the present reality without realizing this. For example Picasso was much more anti-establishment in his pink or blue periods than he was in his cubist period. Today artists throw themselves at realities that no longer exist. They fight against a bourgeois-mindedness that has not existed since the nineteenth century and not at all against the triumphant utilitarianism and pragmatism that is omnipresent today.

According to you modern art is "split asunder". What kind of discontent has caused this to happen ?

Take Dali's painting in one instance, there is his Christ which for me is one of the most beautiful crucifixion paintings ever. Then we have cubism as the other instance. These two examples show how art is split. The first represents the helplessness and suffering of man in the face of technology and second is a work that reflects the chilling perfection of the technological system.

How has modern art become an epiphenomenon of the technological system ?

I believe that most of this modern art is intended to be used in the technological world. I think that all the music and films that are produced for the television is very characteristic of the way art is considered as a sort of technological output. No-one can avoid this. This art has no other reality than to satisfy the imperious demands of a technological apparatus.

---

[1] As an experienced swimmer surfaces from a dive.
They emerge from death as from a dream
[2] My father this sweet-smiling hero
Followed by a lone hussard whom he love above all other
For his great courage and mighty form
Rode out over the battle field all strewn with corpses
Over which the long night was falling.

NAME INDEX

—A—

Adler Alfred 48
ANC 96
Armstrong Louis 129
Aron Robert 8; 10; 15
Aubigné Agrippa d' 130
Audeguil Fernand 13; 77; 78

—B—

Bach Johann Sebastian VIII; 91; 95; 98; 99; 129
Bakunin Michael 8; 101
Balzac 52
Barth Karl 5; 17; 46; 85; 99; 101; 104; 110
Barthes Roland 15
Bataille Georges VII; 59; 67
Baudelaire Charles 131
Beethoven Ludwig von 95
Benzacar Joseph 53
Berdiaeff Nicholas 8
Bergamin 16
Bergson Henri 52
Boiteux Marcel 3
Bonnard Roger VIII; 18; 69; 73
Bonnefoy Yves 131
Bourdieu Pierre 15; 16; 82; 89
Breitmayer Paulo 60
Breuil Roger 11
Briand Aristide 35
Bruckner Pascal 15

—C—

Calvin 46; 47; 78
Chaban Delmas Jacques 14; 75
Char René 131
Charbonneau Bernard VII; VIII; 3; 4; 5; 6; 7; 8; 9; 10; 11; 12; 13; 15; 16; 17; 24; 28; 29; 53; 54; 59; 60; 61; 62; 63; 64; 65; 66; 67; 70; 72; 75; 77; 78; 82; 85; 86; 91; 92; 93; 94; 117; 118; 119
Charrier Yves 87; 88
Chevalley Claude 3; 67
Claudel Paul 51

Claudius-Petit 18
Claudius-Petit Eugène 78; 80
Clémenceau Georges 35
Colletti Lucio 52
Cruse Edmond 45
Cusin Gaston 13

—D—

Dali Salvador VIII; 129; 131; 132; 134
Dandieu Arnaud 3; 8; 10; 63
Daniel-Rops Henri 17; 18
Daudin (Mrs Charbonneau) Henriette 11
de Dietrich Suzanne 105
de Fabrègues Jean 17
de Gaulle Charles 14; 18
de Holbach Paul Henri 50
de La Rocque colonel 9
de Lattre de Tassigny 71
de Leconte de Lisle Charles Marie 52
de Rougemont Denis 15; 64
de Vigny Alfred 52
Delacroix Eugène VIII; 129; 130
Delaunay Gabriel 13; 78; 80; 82
Delpech 72
Diltey Wilhelm 1
Dubuffet Jean 132
Duverger Maurice VII; 14; 49; 55

—E—

Ellul (née Lensvelt) Yvette VIII; 91
Ellul Joseph (father of Jacques Ellul) 2
Eschenauer 33; 35; 80
Esprit V; VII; 8; 9; 10; 11; 12; 16; 17; 28; 53; 54; 59; 62; 63; 64; 65; 66; 67; 93

—F—

Farbos Pierre 42; 43; 46
Fauconnet Luc 88
Ferré Léo VIII; 129
Fouchier Pierre 60
Frankfurt School 7; 16
Frenay Henri 18; 75; 80
Freud Sigmund 48

—G—

Gary Romain 20
Gay Peter 16

Name Index

Germain Pierre 4
Giono Jean 7
Goethe Johann Wolfgang von VII; 49; 51; 52
Gouin Jean 64
Guéhenno Jean 26
Guénon René 67

—H—

Hassan II of Morocco VIII; 91
Hébert Yves 4
Heidegger Martin 7; 16; 82
Henriot Philippe 55
Hérault 43
Hitler Adolf VII; 22; 37; 59; 63; 98; 106
Hitlerjugend 59
Hugo Victor VIII; 129; 130; 131
Huxley Aldous 4; 14; 63; 126

—I—

Illich Ivan 15; 27
Imberti Jean 17; 62; 64
Inkatha 96

—J—

Janicaud Dominique 7
Jeune Droite 8
Jeune République 18; 56; 57
Jeunesses Patriotes 8; 17; 53; 55
Jèze Gaston VII; 49; 56
Jung Carl Gustav 48
Jünger Ernst 7; 92

—K—

Kastler Alfred 4
Kierkegaard Sören VII; 4; 5; 16; 49; 52; 85; 113
Klee Paul VIII; 129; 133
Kressman (René et Edouard) 45

—L—

Laval Pierre 73
Le Bras, le professeur 73
Le Pen Jean-Marie VII; 27; 30
Léca 55
Lensvelt (Mrs Ellul) Yvette 11
Loubet del Bayle 8; 18

—M—

Malraux André 18; 56
Mancipium 70
Marc Alexandre 8; 10; 15; 57; 63; 64
Marcel Gabriel 3; 16
Marcuse 27
Marx Karl VII; 4; 5; 19; 24; 49; 50; 52; 53; 85
Maulnier Thierry 17
Maurras Charles 25
Maxence Jean-Pierre 17
Mendès France Pierre VII; 33; 36
Mendès Marthe (mother of Jacques Ellul) 2
Merle Marcel 97
Michaux Henri 131
Michelangelo VIII; 129; 130
Mitterrand François 18
Mounier Emmanuel VII; 8; 10; 11; 12; 59; 61; 62; 65; 66; 67
Mouvement de libération nationale (MNL) 13
Mozart Wolfgang Amadeus VIII; 91; 95; 98; 99; 129
MSI (the Italian neofascist party) 98
Mumford Lewis 63
Musset Alfred 131
Mussolini Benito 56

—N—

Nietzsche Friedrich 21
Nieztsche 57
Noël Marie 131
Nordon Didier 16

—O—

Obrenovic' (ancestor of Ellul) VII; 33; 34
Ordre Nouveau VII; 3; 8; 10; 11; 17; 59; 63; 64

—P—

Palmier Jean-Michel 16
Péguy Charles VIII; 102; 129; 131; 133
Pétain Philippe 71
Picasso Pablo 133
Plato 52
Pleven René 36
Poplawski, dean of law school 79; 100
Prévost Pierre 67
Proudhon Joseph 8; 18; 85; 86

Name Index

—R—

Rathenau Walter 6; 7; 16
Ricoeur Paul 7
Rimbaud Arthur 131
Rödel Henri 56
Rousseau Jean-Jacques 107
Roy Christian 11; 17; 18

—S—

Saint-John Perse Alexis 131
Sartre Jean-Paul VIII; 15; 27; 91; 97
Sauvy Alfred 62
Schubert Franz 95
Schumann Robert 95
Serres Michel 15
Seurin Jean-Louis V; 18
Sombart Werner 8
Spengler Oswald 6; 16
Stendahl 52
Sternhell Zeev 8
Stockhausen Karl Heinz 131

—T—

Tacitus VII; 49; 51
Taittinger Pierre 17
Tocqueville Alexis de 6; 86

—U—

Uriage School VII; 59; 67

—V—

Vahanian Gabriel 18
Villon François VIII; 129; 130
Vizioz Henri VIII; 18; 69; 73
Voltaire 34
Von Salomon Ernst 7

—W—

Wandervogel VII; 59
Weber Max 8; 89
Weill Kurt 130
Weyembergh Maurice 16
Winock Michel 8

Jacques Ellul

—X—

Xenakis Yannis 131

International Jacques Ellul Society

The International Jacques Ellul Society was founded in 2000 along with its French-language sister-society, the *Association Internationale Jacques Ellul*. The IJES links together scholars and friends of various specializations, vocations, backgrounds, and nations, who share a common interest in the legacy of Jacques Ellul (1912-94), long time professor at the University of Bordeaux.

The three objectives of the IJES are (1) to preserve and disseminate Ellul's literary and intellectual heritage, (2) to extend his penetrating social critique, especially concerning technology, and (3) to extend his theological and ethical research with its special emphases on hope and freedom.

The IJES maintains a web site—*www.ellul.org*—as a resource for those interested in Jacques Ellul. It is also the publisher of the semi-annual *Ellul Forum,* a journal founded in 1988. For more information, visit the web site or contact IJES, P.O. Box 5365, Berkeley CA 94705 USA. Tel/fax: 510-653-3334

www.ingramcontent.com/pod-product-compliance
Lightning Source LLC
Chambersburg PA
CBHW070915160426
43193CB00011B/1462